D1251448

THE JEWISH PEOPLE

HISTORY • RELIGION • LITERATURE

THE JEWISH PEOPLE

HISTORY • RELIGION • LITERATURE

JUDAISM AND ST. PAUL

TWO ESSAYS

C[LAUDE] G. MONTEFIORE

ARNO PRESS
A New York Times Company
NEW YORK • 1973

Reprint Edition 1973 by Arno Press Inc.

Reprinted from a copy in
The Princeton Theological Seminary Library

THE JEWISH PEOPLE: History, Religion, Literature
ISBN for complete set: 0-405-05250-2
See last pages of this volume for titles.

Manufactured in the United States of America

Library of Congress Cataloging in Publication Data

Montefiore, Claude Joseph Goldsmid, 1858-1938.
    Judaism and St. Paul.

    (The Jewish people: history, religion, literature)
    Reprint of the 1914 ed. published by M. Goschen, Lon-
don.
    1. Judaism. 2. Paul, Saint, apostle. I. Title.
II. Series.
BM535.M568 1973   296.3   73-2222
ISBN 0-405-05284-7

JUDAISM
AND ST. PAUL

JUDAISM AND ST. PAUL

TWO ESSAYS

BY

C. G. MONTEFIORE

LONDON

MAX GOSCHEN LTD.

20 GREAT RUSSELL STREET, W.C.

1914

TO

ARNOLD PAGE

DEAN OF PETERBOROUGH

IN

GRATITUDE AND AFFECTION

PREFATORY NOTE

THE two essays of which the present little volume is composed were written some months ago, but various circumstances have prevented an earlier publication. I am indebted to several friends for many suggestions and corrections, for which I now tender them my grateful thanks.

It should perhaps be stated that the first essay deliberately omits the consideration of a number of questions and topics which, though closely connected with its main subject, have been so fully discussed and set forth (from different and opposing points of view) that it seemed unnecessary to repeat what has been already so ably and learnedly said by others. Hence a certain allusiveness in the treatment, which students of St. Paul will readily forgive, but which will yet, I trust, not render the essay unintelligible to the general reader.

As regards the second essay, I should say that I have no call or commission to speak for Liberal Judaism as a whole. And as a growing and living faith, young in years, though confident of a long life, Liberal Judaism is still, in many matters, engaged in thinking out its own position. My contributions, both here and elsewhere, are those of a private individual, who in some things is perhaps more conservative, and in some more radical, than other Jews no less ardently Jewish and Liberal than he. In particular, my attitude towards the New Testament, its central hero and his greatest apostle, though I am vain enough to think that it will be the common attitude of Liberal Judaism tomorrow, is hardly its common and usual attitude to-day.

I have only to add that a few paragraphs towards the end of the first essay are taken from an article of mine upon St. Paul, published in the *Jewish Quarterly Review* many years ago.

C. G. M.

January, 1914.

CONTENTS

                                                    PAGE

THE GENESIS OF THE RELIGION
    OF ST. PAUL   -   -   1

THE RELATION OF ST. PAUL TO
    LIBERAL JUDAISM -   -   131

APPENDIX   -   -   -   221

THE GENESIS OF THE RELIGION
OF ST. PAUL

EVERYTHING which is connected, or which may be linked up, with a great original genius like Paul has its interest and fascination. It may be doubted whether this interest and fascination can ever pass away. For Paul had too deep an effect upon the thought and religion of the Western world for his personality and opinions ever to become matters of indifference to all those who fall within the limits of European influence and civilisation. His doctrine, as we find it expressed and implied in those of the Epistles which are generally recognised as genuine, will, I should imagine, constantly invite fresh attempts at exposition and criticism. The ingenuity and learning of the commentator will be called into play generation after generation, and each age will perchance fondly fancy that it has advanced a little

B

nearer to the meaning of the Apostle, and has thrown some new and fuller light upon those numerous dark places which, from their very obscurity, attract the ingenious interpreter, as the honey-laden flower attracts the industrious bee. But not only his doctrine and actual words draw men to them. We would fain know all that we can about his spiritual history; the antecedents of his doctrine; his mental and moral character; the events of his life. What sort of man was Paul before the conversion near Damascus, before the great outward or inward event which changed his outlook, his beliefs, and his activities? What had he felt and experienced? By what inner processes, if at all, was the conversion led up to and prepared? What were the earlier influences to which Paul had been subjected? What was the exact nature of his environment so far as it affected his religious development—his faith and his doubts (if doubts he had), his yearnings, his struggles, his ideals? More specifically, we would fain know what sort of Jew this man Paul actually was, seeing that several Judaisms, all more or less fluid and growing, existed in the first century, and that Paul may have been influenced by more than one of them. How old was Paul when Jesus died ? And lastly, we would dearly like to be told, with definiteness and detail, how much Paul knew of other religions and of other religious thought outside his own.

To all these fascinating and perplexing questions full and certain answers can never be obtained. We must be satisfied with arguments and probabilities and even with ignorance. Yet this last is that with which we shall never be satisfied, and hence the constant search, the renewed enquiry.

To-day we flatter ourselves, and not without justification, that we can add a little to our knowledge, and here and there can correct the interpretations of the past. Indubitably the great scholars have found out a great deal more than preceding generations knew of the Hellenistic world, of its thought, its religion (doctrine and cultus included), and its literature. Inscriptions and papyri have yielded up many a secret. Whole religions, so to speak, have been revivified, and forgotten phases of thought and aspiration have been discovered and revealed. It is also not inaccurate to say that our knowledge of the Judaism, or, as we had perhaps better say, of the Judaisms of the first century, has also been increased within the last twenty or thirty years. Apocalyptic and Hellenistic 'Judaisms' have been extensively and intensively studied, with the result that they, or their literary products, are known much better and more fully than has hitherto been the case. And of Palestinian or early Rabbinic Judaism it may be said that we realize better the limits of our knowledge ; we realize how meagre is its literary remains ; and we realize also how the purest Rabbinic Judaism of 50 A.D., whether in doctrine or in the type of average believer which it produced, may not have been wholly the same as the Rabbinic Judaism of 500. Then again we have also come to perceive that, as regards the Jewish world of 50 A.D., these divisions, Rabbinic, Apocalyptic, Hellenistic, are not water-tight or cut and dry. They fuse and mingle with each other, and in the living personalities of 50 A.D. there must have been many combinations in which two, or even all three, of these divisions were represented in different proportions and in varying degrees.

Lastly, we all believe ourselves to be, and perhaps a few of us—such as Loisy or Lake or Herford—actually are, more impartial than our fathers, and therefore better able to perceive and describe the Truth. Some of us perhaps are able to do more adequate justice *both* to Gentile *and* Jew, *both* to Jesus *and* the Pharisee, *both* to Paul *and* the Rabbis, *both* to the Gospel *and* the Law. Some have come to believe that, even in the first century, there were many saints among those who accepted Jesus and many saints among those who rejected him ; many holy men among those who followed and appreciated Paul, and many holy men among those who disliked and attacked him. Some of us have come to realize that there are varieties of saintliness, different types of righteousness, and that one must not judge any religion by the picture drawn of it by an antagonist or a convert. Some of us believe that in religious quarrels (as in other quarrels) there is something to be said for both sides, and that each party, and the religion of each party, are much better than they are painted by the other. Some of us have learnt to realize that there are many pathways which lead to God, and they are fain to believe that the Father of all is well pleased to accept the very varying conceptions of Himself, and the very varying conceptions of His relation to man, worked out by Jew and by Christian, with equal indulgence, and perhaps with the same loving condescension of perfect goodness and perfect understanding. For none are impartiality and knowledge and sympathy more urgently necessary than for Paul and his antagonists. None more greatly require detachment of mind and a comprehensiveness of vision. And dangerous capacity though imagination be, it is surely necessary for those working hypotheses without which we cannot at present get on, that some grains of imagination should fill up and illumine the many gaps in our knowledge.

Hitherto the large majority of scholars who have studied Paul most deeply have been unsympathetic to his antagonists and to Rabbinic Judaism. They have also been somewhat lacking in first-hand knowledge. Rabbinic Judaism seems to be the one department of learning about which many great scholars have been willing to make assertions without being able to read the original authorities, or to test the references and statements of the writers whom they quote.[1] Such a willingness is the more surprising when one remembers that these scholars are all more or less inclined, whether from training or environment, from faith or from tradition, to be sympathetic towards

---

[1] "Als rühmliche Ausnahmen sind in dieser Beziehung Dalman Strack Wuensche, und von englischen Gelehrten, Taylor and Herford zu nennen. Was auf allen andern Gebieten als eine selbstverständliche Voraussetzung der Forschung gilt muss also hier als selténer Vorzug besonders hervorgehoben werden."—*Felix Perles in Archiv für Religionswissenschaft* (1913) *p*, 589, *Vol*. xvi.

Paul and unsympathetic to the Rabbis. If a man knew that he had a bit of a bias against Plato, would he not be careful, if he meant to write a book about the Platonic philosophy, to study Plato very thoroughly? Would he be content to use a mere text book about Plato, more especially if he knew that the text book was composed by a man who had the same kind of bias as his own?[1] If a scholar quotes at second hand a statement about Confucius, it does not much matter, for he has no reason not to be perfectly impartial as regards Confucius and Confucianism. But when the quotation concerns the Law or the Talmud, this impartiality does not exist. There is almost always, or up till now there has almost always been, an unconscious prejudice against Talmud, Rabbi and Law. A standard of excellence or rightness has been set up from childhood in the scholar's mind, and this standard has been partly formed by one of the very parties in the dispute which the

---

[1] The allusion is to the still too habitual use of the one-sided and biassed book of Ferdinand Weber's Jüdische Theologie. (*2nd ed. 1897.*)

scholar has to analyze and to describe. Surely, impartiality being thus so difficult to obtain, it would be thought that the scholar would at least seek to provide a make-weight by a superabundance of knowledge. And yet in the very department where knowledge is most desirable, the scholar appears to think it least necessary. He has his text book and a few translations, and he is content. What wonder that the spirit of Rabbinic Judaism should escape him? The very word 'spirit' in connection with that religion would strike him as misplaced and ridiculous! For is not Rabbinic Judaism all letter and no spirit?

On the other side, the Jewish scholar has hitherto shown little capacity for appreciating Paul. The fact is easily explicable and pardonable, but remains a fact none the less. A merely defensive attitude, or a merely combative attitude, prevents the possibility of comprehensive vision and sympathetic impartiality. The Jewish scholar is always wanting to show that Paul was unjust to the Law, and that his charges do not apply. He is probably quite correct, but such proofs do not take one very far in a positive understanding and appreciation of the author of the Epistle to the Romans. Paul may have been unjust to the Law, but he may be a great religious genius none the less ; he may have had some important things to say to the men of his own day, and may have even some important things to say to us. You will never get to understand a book or a religion, if you are always on the look out for its worse side, for its faults or errors and crudities ; if you are always trying to contrast it with the ideal of religious perfection which your own religion seems to you to possess. To pick holes is a poor and easy task ; it carries one a very little way. And yet it seems a delightful occupation both for Christian and Jew. The right thing is surely to ask : What is there in this religion or in this religious book which has caused men and women to die for it, or to live through it noble and holy lives? Moreover,

although the bulk of the Pauline Epistles
is so tiny as compared with the huge
corpus of Rabbinical literature, it may
yet be doubted whether the Jewish scholar
has given the adequate time for their
proper comprehension. For, after all, the
Epistles are extremely difficult, and the
very fact that Jewish prejudices are apt
to be aroused, and that the Jewish mind is
inclined to be rubbed up the wrong way, at
the first and second reading, make a third
and a fourth reading so exceedingly desirable. One of the greatest Rabbinic scholars
of his age, Dr. Schechter, whose books
should be read again and again by all who
wish to know what the ' spirit ' of the Rabbinic religion really was, has clearly made no
vigorous and painful effort to appreciate
Paul. He speaks of him and of his commentators with a certain hauteur and irony
which are at first amusing and perhaps
rarely unjustified, but which, when repeated
too often, become at last a little boring, and
which, at any rate, do not illuminate.
' The apostle himself,' he says ' I do not

profess to understand.'[1]   Has he, one won-
ders, ever fairly tried ?   Has he sat down
with the Greek text and a couple of good
commentaries before him, and laboriously
read through the main Epistles three times
running ?   He ventures on this curious
alternative : ' Either the theology of the
Rabbis must be wrong, its conception of
God debasing, its leading motives material-
istic and coarse, and its teachers lacking in
enthusiasm and spirituality, or the Apostle
to the Gentiles is quite unintelligible.'   I
believe that this alternative is both unnecessary and inaccurate.   The theology of
the Rabbis is none of these dreadful things
which Dr. Schechter says it must be if Paul
should be intelligible, and, on the other
hand, we can go far, and later generations
will, I hope, go further, in the understanding
of Paul.

The only possible value of the present
essay is that it is written by one who, though
unlearned, has a profound admiration for
Paul, and is also convinced that many of

---

[1] Schechter—'*Some Aspects of Rabbinic Theology.*'(1909)*p*.18.

those who rejected and scorned his teaching were noble men of the deepest religious faith and livers of fair and saintly lives. While readily acknowledging that Paul was a great original genius, and that there is no reason to believe that any one of his Jewish antagonists approached him in greatness, in originality or in genius, the present writer feels none the less convinced that among those very antagonists were many who loved God no less passionately than he, and were no less loyal to the highest that they knew.

It is not a statement or exposition of Paul's teaching and religious position that I want to give in this essay. Incidentally I shall have to speak of some of his teachings and of his religious position. But chiefly I want to touch once more upon that well-worn subject of Paul's religious antecedents—his religious history and opinions before his conversion—and of his relation to the Judaisms of his age and time. The main question in my mind is this : How far was Paul, up to his conversion, a Rabbinic Jew ?

Was Rabbinic Judaism the religion which he had known, believed in, and practiced ?

Let us assume, for the moment, that it was. In order, then, to gain some sort of an idea of what Paul's religion was before his conversion, we should have to start with a description of Rabbinic Judaism as it existed about the year 30 or 50 A.D. Paul was, indeed, in no case an average or ordinary Jew : even before his conversion he was a genius, and not an average or ordinary personality. Still, we might assume, even if his religion had something peculiar, distinctive and personal about it, that nevertheless a full and impartial description of Rabbinic Judaism of the year 30 would, to a large extent, be a description of the religion of Paul.

But now comes a great and crucial difficulty. Can the Rabbinic Judaism of 30 or 50 A.D. be adequately described ? Have we enough material from which to do so ? This is doubtful. The great bulk of Rabbinic literature is much later. The other Jewish material, dating from about 100 B.C. to

100 A.D. which we actually possess, or which, let us rather say, may be probably relegated to these two hundred years, is the work of writers whose relation to Rabbinic Judaism is often doubtful and disputed. It is, therefore, somewhat precarious to attempt a picture of Rabbinic Judaism as it existed in men's minds and hearts and lives during, shall we say, the first half of the first century A.D. It is not even easy to say whether the Rabbinic Judaism of 30 was ' better ' or ' worse ' (according to the religious standards of to-day) than the Rabbinic Judaism of 300. Either view has been maintained, yet perhaps less from the evidence than from some reason or preconception outside this evidence and disconnected with it. But one thing at least we can do, and this provisional course I propose to take. We know the Rabbinic Judaism of 300 or 500 in some detail. And so, provisionally, we will waive the question as to the relation of Rabbinic Judaism of 500 or 300 to that of 50 or 30. We will take the Rabbinic Judaism of 500,

the Rabbinic Judaism of the Talmud and of the Midrash, so far as such a phrase is reasonable and legitimate. And without asking now how far, or whether, such a Judaism existed in 50, let us put the question : What was the relation of Paul's religion before his conversion to *this* Rabbinic Judaism ? How far was his religion, before the event at Damascus, the same as, or different from, that of any ordinary and average representative of Rabbinic Judaism ? How far was Paul (in the sense which the words would bear in the year 500), a typical Rabbinic Jew ? When these questions have been answered, the further and more difficult problem can still be raised : Was the Rabbinic Judaism of 500 the same as the Rabbinic Judaism of 50, and, if not, in what did the one differ from the other ? Did the earlier differ from the later Rabbinic Judaism just in those very ways and points as to make it quite reasonable to argue that, though Paul could not be fairly described as a typical Rabbinic Jew of the 500 or 300 type, he can rightly be described according to the type of 50 and 30 ?   A brief and 'undocumented' answer to this second series of questions must perhaps be risked here : a more detailed or definite answer must be ultimately given by the scholars. Nevertheless (paradoxical as it may sound) the really interesting questions, and theologically the more important questions, are contained in the first series and not in the second. The reason may become apparent later on.

The reader will already perceive that the present writer is going to argue that Paul's pre-Christian religion must have been, in many important points, very unlike the religion of a representative Rabbinic Jew of the year 500. But, in spite of Dr. Schechter, that does not make him unintelligible. For the question of the relation of the Rabbinic Judaism of 500 to that of 50 remains over. Moreover, there were other branches of Judaism existing in 50 over and above the purest Rabbinic type. And, lastly there were religious influences to which Paul

c

may have been subjected, and religious ideas with which he may have been familiar, which were not Jewish at all.

To explain adequately what we find, and what we do not find, in Paul's Christian writings, we must, as I believe, assume, first, that the Judaism which he knew, and in which he believed, was in many ways different from the Rabbinic Judaism of 500, and, secondly, that he had been subject, and had become susceptible, to those outside influences which were not Jewish at all. As regards the second assumption, the reader will perceive that I have fallen a victim to the views of such scholars as Reitzenstein and Loisy. But I am much more concerned with the first assumption than with the second. And for the following reason which will also give the reason and the justification for the present short essay.

Up till recently, the general view has been that, even if Paul could be rightly called a Hellenistic Jew, or even if he had been subject to certain Hellenistic influences, yet in so far as his Judaism was concerned,

that Judaism, in all the big fundamentals,
closely resembled the Judaism of ' the
Rabbis.'   It was further assumed that the
Judaism of 50 was much the same in its
legalism, its externality, its ' burdens,' its
self-righteousness, etc., etc., as the Judaism
of 500.   So Paul's pre-Christian Judaism, in
all the big fundamentals, closely resembled
the Rabbinic Judaism of 500 no less than
the Rabbinic Judaism of 50.   Paul's own
statements seemed to demand this view.
Does he not say that he ' had advanced in
the Jews' religion beyond many of mine
own age among my countrymen, being more
exceedingly zealous for the traditions of my
fathers ' ?[1]   And again, in one of his last
utterances, does he not say that he was 'as
touching the Law, a Pharisee ; as touching
the righteousness which is in the Law, found
blameless ' ?[2]   And is there not a marked
tendency now-a-days, even among great
scholars like Lake and Harnack, to believe
what is found in the book of the Acts, and
does not Paul say in that book that he was

---

[1] Galatians i, 14.   [2] Phillippians iii, 5, 6.

brought up in Jerusalem, at the feet of Gamaliel, and ' instructed according to the strict manner of the law of our fathers, being zealous for God even as ye all are this day'?[1] Thus it was Rabbinic Judaism which was supposed to be the 'Jewish background' and antecedent of Paul's theology. Indeed, rags and tatters—ugly, disconnected remainders—of the old religion were supposed occasionally to peep through. And these 'remainders' were exceedingly convenient, and supplied a delightful explanation. Anything you disliked or disagreed with in Paul's writings, any weakness or crudity in argument or theory, any superstition or credulity, you called a Rabbinic survival, and the whole matter was explained, excused and set aside. All the good things, or the things which you happened to think good and true, were new and original and Christian and Pauline ; all the bad things, or the things which you happened to think bad or false, were survivals and Jewish and Rabbinic. One can well understand that

---

[1] Acts xxii, 3.

it will need a great deal of effort if scholars should have to discard so simple and so pleasant a phraseology.

If Rabbinic Judaism was the religious antecedent of Paul, then Paul knew all about Rabbinic Judaism. He could criticise it as one who had been within its pale, and had lived the life which it demands. And although a convert rarely criticises fairly the religion which he has left, still it makes a great difference whether Paul left Rabbinic Judaism or some other kind of Judaism, which, in the very points wherein he criticised it, was not Rabbinic (as the Rabbinic Judaism of 300 or 500 is 'Rabbinic') at all. If he was not only a convert, but did not even know Rabbinic Judaism, his criticism and attacks are of no value *as regards that particular religion*. He was then certainly not the great pathologist (as Wellhausen calls him) of *Rabbinic* Judaism at all. And this conclusion, if I am right in drawing it, would be of considerable importance. For the gruesome horrors and the sad, inevitable religious fiasco of Rabbinic

Judaism (with which many Christian scholars have made us so familiar), are mainly drawn from the criticism of Paul. He said so : he had been through the mill, and he ought to know ! Doubtless the Rabbinic writings have been made to furnish proof that what Paul said was accurate and right. But those writings are so vast and difficult, so easily capable of misinterpretation and false emphasis, that be you Jew or Christian, you can pretty certainly find in them whatever you desire. Exquisite tolerance, arid externalism— given adequate preconception, you can haul up from that sea any kind of fish.

How different will our conclusions have to be if we are driven to believe that Paul's criticisms of Rabbinic Judaism (except one) never come home, simply because his religious ' background '—the Jewish foil for his new Christian doctrine—is not Rabbinic Judaism as we know it from the Rabbinic literature and from Rabbinic life. For those criticisms, it must be remembered, are not intended to be (like the mordant criticisms of Jesus) criticisms of the perversions of Rabbinic Judaism, of the defects of its qualities. He is not a pathologist in that sense, that he lays bare sicknesses, which assume a possible condition of health. For he criticises the whole theory of the Judaism which was opposed to him, its foundations and its outcome.

But all this I admit, is a parenthesis and indeed an anticipation. Let it here suffice to emphasize the fact that hitherto it was Rabbinic Judaism which was supposed to explain Paul (so far as his main and fundamental Jewish antecedents were concerned) and it was Rabbinic Judaism on which he was supposed to throw such searching and unveiling light.

Now to prove the truth of my thesis about Paul and Rabbinic Judaism would need, I am aware, a large book and much learning. I have not the learning, and cannot therefore write the book. Yet sometimes even an unlearned essay may have its uses. So I proceed to an undertaking which is almost absurdly bold. For in the pursuit of the argument, I have now to throw upon the paper a short description of certain essential elements of the Rabbinic religion. I have to give a short summary of Rabbinic Judaism as it would have been exemplified in the religious consciousness of the average and typical Rabbinic Jew. Let the period be when Rabbinic Judaism was fully developed, which we may place at about 500 or even 300 A.D. Still must I waive the delicate and important question how far the Rabbinic religion of 30 or 50 was very different from, or much the same as, the Rabbinic religion of 300 or 500. (If the Roman Catholicism of 1464 or even 1644 was not quite the same as the Roman Catholicism of 1914, it would not be so very surprising). And the final reason why I must make this rash venture and attempt this daring delineation, is that at the back of my mind I have the conviction that, if the religion of Paul before his conversion had been the religion I am now to describe, the conversion itself might well have taken place, but many things in the

Epistle to the Romans could never have been written.

Let us start by trying, in roughest outline, to picture to ourselves the Rabbinic conception of the Deity. For in Rabbinic Judaism everything follows from, and depends upon, this conception. Rabbinic Judaism taught an intensely personal God. To the Rabbinic Jew God was a distinct individuality, separate, though not distant, from the world which He had made. The average believer was not in the least worried by metaphysical considerations concerning the relation of an ' infinite ' God to a universe which is ' outside ' Him. He carried together in his religious consciousness all sorts of ideas, which, though philosophically inconsistent with each other, harmonised religiously exceedingly well. God was the creator and ruler of the world. He was the Father of Israel and of every Israelite ; He was omnipresent ; He was in heaven ; He had no form ; He had no flesh or blood ; He was not ' material ' : nevertheless He could and did ' hear ' every sincere prayer

of all His human children ; He was anxious
to hear it ; He loved to hear it. His throne
was far off on high ; but He was also very
near. He had no material eyes or ears ; but
He saw and knew everything which was
going on, and He concerned Himself greatly
with the fortunes of His people, to whom, as
His most precious gift, He had given His·
perfect and immutable Law.

This simple personal God was great and
awful, but He was also merciful and loving.
He did not delegate His relations with
Israel to any angel or subordinate. Between
Him and every Israelite there was no go-
between, intercessor or mediator. The
child could, and did, go direct to the Father,
and the Father dealt directly with the child.
No human priest, no angelic or divine being,
obtruded on this simple and immediate
relation between the Israelite and his God.
The Rabbinic Jew doubtless believed in
angels. He might even have used a later
phrase, and said, ' In the name of the Lord,
the God of Israel, may Michael be at my
right hand ; Gabriel at my left ; before

me Uriel ; behind me, Raphael ' ; but such expressions would have had little value for him. They were undogmatic. These angels were mere servants of God, and the Rabbinic Jew never thought it necessary to ask an angel to present his supplications to the divine Lord both of angels and of men. For a hundred times in which he made mention of God, there was only one in which he alluded to an angel.

God was, as I have said, mighty and awful, but He was also kindly and pitiful. His relations with Israel and with all Israelites are similiar to the relations of a human father to his children. As a human father grieves sorely over the faults of his children, and longs for them to be sorry for their offences, so too with God. He grieves bitterly over the faults (and the calamities to which these faults have led) of His beloved people. He longs for their repentance. His own glory is intimately bound up with theirs. His kingship is involved in, and depends upon, their acceptance and proclamation of it. So too, like a human

father, God rewards and punishes ; He
chastises and He forgives ; above all, He
cares for His children's welfare ; He loves
them ; He wants them to be happy and
good. And He has provided them a
means by which happiness and goodness
may be secured—a means which, at the
same time, reveals and makes manifest His
own kingship and glory. This means is the
Law. To follow the precepts of the Law
means joy on earth and joy in the life to
come. Joy on earth consists in fulfilling
the commands of the perfect God, who
has chosen out Israel from all the other
peoples of the world and has given them
His Law. This gift constituted Israel's
special duty and special privilege, and every
separate injunction is duty and privilege in
one. The fulfilment of the divine precepts
should also lead to a happy life in the
ordinary sense of the word—to earthly
welfare and prosperity. For various reasons
this result by no means always follows,
but the joy in the *doing*, the glad consciousness of sonship in the execution of

the commandments—these are always to
be obtained.

But are there not *many* commandments,
some ' moral,' some ' ceremonial ' ?   Yes,
there are.   The more commands, the more
honour ; the more injunctions, the more
privilege ; the more precepts, the more
gladness ; the more laws, the more means
for self-purification and self-control.   The
many statutes lead to santification.   No one
individual can fulfil them all.   Some of the
laws relate to sacrifices.   But the Temple is
destroyed, and even while it stood, by no
means all the laws concerned every Jew.
Some are only for priests, some for Levites;
some for women ; some for the king.   But
a fair number remain, and the Rabbinic
Jew, in a manner unpleasing to modern
liberal Jews, daily thanks God that he is a
man and not a woman, because men have
more commandments to fulfill than women.
Greater privilege has, therefore, been given
to them ; greater opportunity for the
purest joy.   The core and essence of the
Rabbinic religion are contained in that one

familiar phrase, 'the joy of the commandments.' Nor is anything more significant
and revealing of the real inwardness of that
religion than the simple fact that the same
Hebrew word, which in the Old Testament
period means commandment and nothing
but commandment, came in the Rabbinic
period to mean privilege (or honour) as
well. We are wont to think of ' the Law '
as a series of enactments, upon the violation of which, punishment would ensue.
To the Rabbinic Jew the Law was something quite different. It is true that for
its violation you would be punished. It is
true that for its observance you would be
rewarded. It is true that it was your duty
and obligation to obey it, that it stood, in
a sense, outside and above you, threatening
you with penalties, if also inciting you with
rewards. But it was far more than a mere
arbitrary code which you had to obey, if you
wanted to be prosperous and escape a whip-
ping, as a schoolboy must obey the, to him,
often arbitrary rules of his irresponsible
schoolmaster. The Rabbinic Jew knew why

the Law had been given. He knew that it came from a God, who was perfect in righteousness and in love. He knew that it had been given him for his own good. In the execution of the Law's injunctions his own nature would be purified and hallowed. In the observance of its enactments he would find life, happiness, satisfaction, peace. It was not, so to speak, God in His capacity as severe judge or as awful master who had given to the Israelites His Law, it was God as loving and merciful. It was the grace of God which was made visible in the Law.

To the Rabbinic Jew, who conformed to average and type, the observance of the Law was in no wise a burden. How should it be so ? Suppose you *really* believe in a ' personal ' God who is perfectly wise and perfectly good. Suppose you also believe that this perfectly good and perfectly wise God has entered into special relations with your race or community, and that, through His accredited messenger, He has told you to fulfil certain moral and ceremonial laws to the best of your ability. Suppose He has

told you that these laws are *His* laws, and
that in the observance of them you will find
satisfaction and joy, the highest life on earth
and the most blissful life hereafter.   It
seems *prima facie* unlikely that, with this
belief, you will find the fulfilment of the laws
a burden.   And, as a matter of fact, the
great majority of the Jewish evidence goes
to show that, from the end of the first
century at any rate, the laws were not a
burden, but a delight. Moreover in the year
300 or 500 (whatever may have been the
case in 30 or 50), there were not really so
very many of them after all !   All the talk
in the text books of the immense number,
multiplicity and elaboration of the enactments which the ordinary Israelite had to
fulfil is *probably* much exaggerated even for
the year 50 ; for the year 500 it is so undoubtedly. The compulsion of the Law was
chiefly felt in two directions—the Sabbath
and food. There were very many things
which you might not do upon the Sabbath,
but you soon learnt what they were, and if
there is one thing more certain than another

it is that the Sabbath was a joy. There
were numerous laws about food, but some
concerned the butcher, others the women
who cooked ; those which remained were
easily acquired and remembered. These
food laws, doubtless, made, and were intended to make, the intercourse between
Jew and Gentile difficult, unpleasant, or
even impossible, but the average Jew did
not desire any social intercourse with
persons who did not belong to his race and
his religious community.

Again, some bad Jews in every generation
may have pretended to believe, and may
have acted upon the belief, that the strict
observance of the Sabbath and the dietary
laws made an observance of the moral
laws—of justice, charity, compassion—unnecessary and superfluous. Some bad Jews
in every generation may have thought that
the ceremonial laws were more important
than the moral laws. But the average
Rabbinic Jew did not think so. The bad
Jews did not conform to type. They were
the excrescence ; they were not the usual

D

and regular product. They did not represent the 'spirit' of the Rabbinic creed. To the typical, and even to the average, Jew the Law was a joy for which he could thank God in sincerity and in truth.

Rabbinic Judaism did not, as is still too commonly believed, produce a regular crop of proud and self-righteous Jews, upon the one hand, and a regular crop of anxious, scrupulous, timid and despairing Jews upon the other. The evidence against such a supposition for the developed Rabbinic Judaism of 500, and for the Rabbinic Judaism of many subsequent generations, is, I believe, fairly conclusive. A religion, like virtue, may be looked at from one point of view as a mean ; from another, as an excess. Looked at as a mean, Rabbinic Judaism lies in between the two extremes just indicated, and the prevailing type of character which it produced—the *characteristic* type of men which it brought up— lay in between the two opposite extremes, and was wholly different from both. Every religion has its exceptional sinners and its

exceptional saints ; every religion produces
perversions from type, spiritual abortions
and caricatures.   Doubtless Rabbinic Judaism was no exception to this rule.   In
each generation there doubtless existed—
and because they existed it is possible to
say that Rabbinic Judaism produced them
—some proud and self-righteous Jews, some
anxious, scrupulous, timid and despairing
Jews.   I have already observed that in *each*
generation there probably existed some
hypocritical Jews, some who observed the
ceremonial laws and neglected the moral
laws, some whose morality was negative,
conventional and poor.   What religion is
without the defects of its qualities ?   Among
the nominal adherents of every religion
there are some bad men.   But the prevailing
type of character which Rabbinic Judaism
produced was very different.   Its adherents
were neither proud, on the one hand, nor
despairing, upon the other.   They were
both humble and hopeful.   They were,
indeed, taught to believe that the average
and decent-living Israelite would inherit

the world to come, would be ' saved,' to use other and more familiar phraselogy. But they were not taught to believe that this result would follow as the guerdon of their own merits ; it would rather befall them as the effect of God's love and God's grace. They prayed : ' May it be thy will, O Lord our God and God of our fathers, that we may keep Thy statutes in this world, and be worthy to live to witness and inherit happiness and blessing in the days of the Messiah, and in the life of the world to come.' But they also said, and the one sentence was no less sincere than the other, ' We know that we have no good works of our own ; deal with us in charity and loving-kindness, and save us.' God's love for Israel, His love of the repentant sinner, His inveterate tendency to forgiveness, together with the merits of the patriarchs, would amply make up for their own individual deficiencies. Their religion was, therefore, happy and hopeful : happy in the performance, within the limits of human frailty, of the divine commands in this

world, hopeful in the belief of the sure in-
heritance hereafter of the finer and purer
beatitudes of the world to come.[1]

But do all Israelites observe the Law ?
Do they fulfil the injunction of this perfect

---

[1]Dr. Vernon Bartlet in his article on Paul in the new
edition of the Encyclopædia Brittanica does me the honour
of referring to certain old papers of mine in the Jewish
Quarterly Review. A full rejoinder to his criticism is here
impossible. I may, however, allude to one or two points. Dr.
Bartlet says : p. 941, col. 2, ' It is unproven and improbable
that Paul unfairly represents the prevailing tendency in the
Pharisaic Judaism of his own day as " legalistic " in the bad
sense. He is really the one extant witness upon the point as
just defined, if we except certain apocalyptic writings (whose
evidence modern Jews are anxious to discount) like the Apoc-
alypse of Baruch and 4 Ezra, the latter of which suggests that
already the humbling effect of the capture of Jerusalem was
being felt.' Legalistic in the bad sense seems to mean pride
and self-righteousness. Now, first, if Paul is really the one
extant witness, he is a very tainted one. It is very hard to
condemn a whole religion, or a whole number of persons, upon
the unsupported evidence of an enemy. Secondly, all such
Rabbinic material as does exist prior to the destruction of the
Temple, including the oldest portion of the liturgy, points the
other way. Thirdly, and this is the most important consideration, when Rabbinic literature becomes ample, we find,
(a) no prevailing self-righteousness or pride, (b) a full-blown
legalism. What becomes then of the contention that the Law
tended to evil ? Again, it may be true that Paul's universalism
was attained by his anti-legal attitude, but why that should
prove that the Law, or that Law, has a specific virus tending
prevailingly to pride and self-righteousness, I fail to perceive.
Assume that the Rabbinic Jews were particularists, and that
particularism is a sin ; yet why should they not have been
humble towards God ? Millions of Christians have believed
that all non-Christians were doomed to everlasting torments,
and that only Christians of their own type of Christianity
would be saved. Yet they have believed in a God of love,
and have loved him, and have lived lives of piety and
righteousness and humility.

code ? And is not God very angry with them if they transgress any of these excellent precepts, whether moral or ceremonial? It is undoubtedly true that they do not all observe the Law, on the contrary, all, more or less, fail to fulfil its injunctions. And doubtless God is very angry. A few hardened and special sinners violate the injunctions of the Law in open revolt and mockery and wickedness. But the enormous mass of persons violate them through weakness, through the solicitations and temptations of the Evil Inclination, through the attractions of base desire, or through any other form of human frailty. Is not then the whole scheme of things, the entire religious system, broken through and broken down ? Where is God's glory ? Where is man's satisfaction ? Both depend upon the keeping of the Law, and the Law cannot be kept.

Theoretically, no doubt, the Law might be a joy. So it would be in fact, if it could be observed. But the Law itself declares that man is accursed unless he

observe the whole Law, that is, *all* its enactments. To observe all the enactments,
both positive and negative, would mean
that a man would be sinless, whereas it is
notorious that all men sin.   If one has
violated the Law by breaking one of its
enactments, and thus by a single transgression become guilty and ' accursed,'
how can the whole thing be other than a
frightful burden, a constant and gnawing
anxiety ?   The issues are tremendous—
life eternal (to say nothing of earthly happiness) is at stake—the chances of success are
infinitesimal. Untempted angels might keep
the Law, and be happy in its observance.
How can man, solicited and tempted by the
evil inclinations within him (and perhaps
without), be happy when he knows that
failure is practically inevitable ? What use
to have observed commandments a, b, c, d,
if one fails to keep e or f ? For it is the
whole Law which must be observed, and he
who is guilty in one injunction is guilty in
all.   How can a Law which must be observed in all its parts, and which yet cannot

be observed in all its parts, be the gift of God's grace ? Surely it must, on the contrary, be the gift of His anger ! Instead of a privilege, it is a burden ; instead of a joy, it is sorrow and gloom; instead of leading to santification and life, it leads to iniquity and death.

It seems a bad business, but the unsystematic and practical character of Rabbinic Judaism, and the goodness and compassion of the God in whom it believed, were equal to the occasion.

It is true that the Israelite often fails to observe God's commands. He offends both negatively and positively. But he reflects that the Law was given to men, and not to angels. It was given to men for their improvement and santification and joy, and it was given to beings who, by their very constitution and history, were bound to make frequent lapses and to fall often into sin. The Rabbinic Jew did not worry himself much about the theory that the whole Law (with all its enactments) has to be obeyed. He took a practical view of the situation, and one which seemed to harmonize with two fundamental facts, first, that God was kind and merciful and compassionate, and not merely awful and holy and severe; secondly, that the Law had been given for life, and not for death, for good, and not for evil. And the difficulty of the Law must not be exaggerated. The Rabbinic Jew realized that the average man can, and often does, fulfil and observe many divine behests, though there is not a command which he could not fulfil more perfectly and devoutly than is actually the case. Still the Law, in its separate injunctions, is not, in one sense, too hard for him. There is no commandment which he cannot fulfil more or less. It is true that the average man fulfils some, and fails to fulfil others. But (in despite of the theory, and even of the Law's own statement), the scheme of things does not break down because of these partial failures. They were foreseen and provided for. If there were no failures, there could be no improvement, no gradual purification, no advance in holiness. In spite of the failures, the Law leads to life and not to death. In spite of the failures, man can rejoice in the commandments. In spite of the failures, he can feel the Law to be a privilege, and not a burden ; not a gloom, but a joy.

But is not God angry at man's violation of the Law ? Yes, He is very angry. But greater than His anger is His compassion. He helps man to repair his fault. He helps him in the struggle to resist temptation. He helps him when he prays ; and by the gracious gift of repentance He helps him both to conquer his sin and to obtain its forgiveness. God delights in man's repentance. Let a man repent but a very little, and God will forgive very much. For He delights in the exercise of forgiveness far more than in the exercise of punishment. So anxious is God about repentance and forgiveness that He instituted in the perfect Law a day consecrated to both. Man may and can and should repent every day ; God can and does pardon every day. But the day of Atonement is the day on which both man and God are, so to speak, engaged in doing nothing else than repentance and forgiveness, on which, for every sincere and humble penitent, there is offered the chance of a fresh start and the opportunity of a clean slate.

There is, therefore, no need whatever for despair. No injunction of the Law is too difficult for a man to seek to obey it. Every man can obey the Law's behests, though every man (and certainly every average man) is bound to fail in obeying them all, or in obeying them perfectly or entirely. Yet the breaches can be repaired. Human repentance, divine forgiveness ; these are the methods. They are made visible and corporealized in the great and crowning mercy of the Law, the Day of Atonement.

Life is solemn, but not appalling. We are *bound* to obey God's injunctions, but *in* these very injunctions and *in* their fulfilment lie happiness and self-realization. For the Law is 'a tree of life to them that grasp it, and of them that uphold it every one is rendered happy.'

None but the deliberate and determined sinner need fail to 'grasp' it; none but the mocker and the apostate are unable to 'uphold' it. It is not only the perfect who can grasp; it is not only the immaculate who can uphold. Therefore the average man, as well as the saint, can say and can *feel*, ' Its ways are ways of pleasantness, and all its paths are peace.'

Rabbinic Judaism was convinced, as I have said, that for every decent Israelite there was a place in the future world, in 'the life to come.' Only then and only there would he find perfect happiness. Nevertheless, although, as a just punishment of many transgressions, the lot of Israel and of the Israelite upon earth was usually hard and unpleasant, the Rabbinic Jew was anxious to taste such happiness as he could even before he died, and before the resurrection of the dead. Though it may be intended that man is to find nothing but joy hereafter, it is not intended that he is to find nothing but sorrow on earth. That, indeed, may often

be the case, but that is not God's inviolable
and invariable intention.   Man is to be
happy here and now : God has given the
means of happiness even upon earth, and
through earthly and material things.   These
earthly and material things man is to enjoy,
and to hallow, through religion.   Eating and
drinking ; family life ; the daily labour ; the
rest after toil ; the sights of nature ; all these
are to be enjoyed—enjoyed *and sanctified.*
The Rabbinic Jew of 500 doubtless believed
in a devil and in demons : but they did not
play a great part in his religion ; they did
not form a conspicuous portion of his religious dogmas.   They were not determin-
ating or cardinal features of his religious
faith.   Their *rôle* was vague, fluctuating,
indistinct.   They belonged rather to his
superstitions and his folk-lore than to his
religion and his creed.   So, to Rabbinic
Judaism, this world is not bad, but good.
The next world will certainly be much
better, but this world is *good*.   God
created it, and He governs it still.   He has
never withdrawn from its government.   He

has never allowed its government to fall into the hands of any lesser divine being than Himself, still less into the hands of some evil spirit or demon. This world is God's world still, and the Israelite is to enjoy it—temperately, purely—as much as he can. For every enjoyment and *in* every enjoyment he is to render thanks to God the Giver. He is to smell the rose, and to rejoice in its perfume. And he is to say and to feel : ' Blessed art Thou, O Lord, who createst fragrant plants.'

Rabbinic Judaism was a simple religion, but it was preserved from becoming too simple by a strong current of intellectualism. This intellectual side did not, however, display itself in systematic theology and metaphysics ; it was chiefly manifested in the study of the Law, where it spent itself in subtle and often arid discussions, in elaborate legal minutiæ, and in endless casuistical distinctions and hairsplittings. However, valueless the larger portion of this legal study may have been as a contribution to human progress and culture, it is doubtful whether it had much injurious effect upon the actual religious life which was lived by the great mass of the total Jewish population. It passed over their heads, and left them unaffected. Concurrently with the purely legal discussions other kinds of religious output existed also. With the *Halachah* went the *Haggadah*, so that the religious imagination of the teachers was not checked or starved. And a certain valuable idealism was undoubtedly produced by this elaborate and never ending study of the Law. The most honoured people among the Jews were not the rich, but the learned ; not the successful money-maker, but the scholar. A mother's ambition was not that her son should be wealthy, but that he should be wise, wise in the wisdom of the schools. A narrow wisdom ; as regards much of it, a useless wisdom ; a wisdom which produced a literature of which huge portions have little value and little charm. Nevertheless, a wisdom. The consecration of the simple ' material ' joys of life, together with the consecration of the mind and of wisdom, was a special and characteristic feature of Rabbinic Judaism, giving to it a cheerful and healthy idealism that was peculiarly its own.

A joyous, simple religion ; yet also an intellectual and rational religion in its own special way : a happy, spiritual, and even ardent religion, but not a religion which passed constantly and rapidly into mysticism. A religion more usually (to use the now familiar words of William James) of the 'healthy-minded' and of the 'once-born.' A religion which provoked much realisation and love of God ; much delight in His service ; much readiness to live for Him and die for Him ; but which always maintained a vivid and profound distinction between man and God, between the human personality and the divine.[1]

---

[1]This does not mean that there was *no* mysticism among the Rabbis (Dr. Abelson has lately twice over proved the contrary), still less that the Rabbis were not capable of sublime thoughts and profound utterances. Such thoughts and utterances meet us by no means infrequently. I am rather surprised that Dr. Herford in his edition of the Sayings of the Fathers (in the great Oxford Apocrypha and Pseudepigrapha ed. Charles) should say of them (Vol. 2, p. 686) :

A religion of every day and family life, not a religion of celibate asceticism or drastic punishments of the flesh. A religion which taught that God helped man to be good, that He was 'near' and approachable and kind, but which strongly and severely maintained a clear-cut and large distinction between the human child and the divine Father. Rabbinic Judaism was without

---

' The reader who will persevere will find much that is valuable and instructive for the right understanding of the religion and ethics of the Pharisees ; much, also, which, without being either very profound or very sublime, is yet well and wisely said.' Tastes and standards differ, but to my thinking the following adages cannot without injustice be regarded as lacking either in sublimity or profoundness. And the ' Sayings of the Fathers ' is a mere selection of the Rabbinic wisdom:

' Be not like servants who minister to their master upon the condition of receiving a reward.'

' If I am not for myself, who will be for me ? And being for myself, what am I ?'

' Do His will as if it were thy will, that He may do thy will as if it were His will.'

' It is not thy duty to complete the work, but neither art thou free to desist from it.'

' He in whom the spirit of his fellow creatures takes delight, in him the Spirit of the All-present takes delight.'

' The recompense of a precept is a precept, and the recompense of a transgression a transgression.'

' This world is like a vestibule before the world to come ; prepare thyself in the vestibule that thou mayest enter into the hall.'

' Better is one hour of repentance and good deeds in this world than the whole life of the world to come : better is one hour of blissfulness of spirit in the world to come than the whole life of this world.'

E

sacraments and without mysteries. It knew of no rapid change from bad to good by any secret initiation or any second and higher birth. For the most part it taught a gradual progress in goodness and knowledge and the love of God : and if it also realised that there are some who inherit ' the kingdom ' in a moment, such instantaneous success was supposed to be only due to repentance and forgiveness—the repentance of man, the forgiveness of God.

Rabbinic Judaism did not readily produce that mystic temper or soul which seems to find itself afresh by losing itself in God. Its saint does not naturally speak of being in God or of God being in him. He does not conceive that it is no longer the old human ' he,' who, now that the higher life has been won, is really acting and working, but a transfigured and new ' he,' perhaps better to be described as ' God in him ' rather than ' himself.' The rapture, the *abandon*, the ecstasy, of that sort of mystic are not typical of Rabbinic Judaism, though, on the other hand, it is inaccurate to say that within Rabbinic Judaism mysticism had no place at all. But its mysticism was of a different kind. Mysticism can, perhaps, never be altogether foreign to any genuine religion, such as Rabbinic Judaism undoubtedly was. Yet, though the generalisation is, I believe, correct, that mysticism of the order of which the fourth Gospel is so familiar and illustrious an example, was not typical of Rabbinic Judaism, it did not on that account produce a lower level of religious feeling or religious life, and it certainly did not produce less readiness for martyrdom. Nor is its ethical quality lower. All that can justly be said is that its fervour and its ethics, its religious temper and spiritual tone, are generally *other* than those of the mystic who feels himself in God and God in him ; it reaches and enjoys God, it attains its moments of intensest communion with Him, but by a different road and in a different way.

In 500 A.D. Rabbinic Judaism still believed (it believes to-day) in the advent of a Messiah and of the Messianic age. But it did not teach that that age was coming soon. The Messiah and his age were relegated to a distant and indefinite future, much as they are to-day, much as the Second Advent is to-day by an orthodox and old-fashioned Protestant. And the Messiah was to be a man ; not a divine or semi-divine being, already pre-existent in ' heaven,' but a human descendant of Davidic stock, who should be born as other men were born, and only differ from other men by his superior righteousness and power.

Such were (in briefest outline), so far as I can make out, the main characteristics of Rabbinic Judaism. But one important point has been so far left out, or rather a point which is of grave importance in one respect, but not of grave importance in another. The religion I have ventured to describe in these rough and clumsy strokes was the religion of the Rabbinic Jew to-wards his God and towards the members of his community and race. But what about the big world outside ? What about the Gentile, the non-Jew in race and the non-

Jew in religion ?   Here we draw near to the one really sore point, the one grave deficiency of the Rabbinic religion.

It cannot truthfully be ignored or denied that the great outstanding fault of Rabbinic Judaism was its particularism. The relation of God to Israel was other than His relation to the world at large. It was not denied that there were a righteous few among the heathen, and the deepest hope of Rabbinic Judaism was expressed and crystallized in the famous prayer, which is still read week by week in every orthodox Synagogue :

' We therefore hope in Thee, O Lord our God, that we may speedily behold the glory of Thy might, when Thou will remove the abominations from the earth, and the idols will be utterly cut off, when the world will be perfected under the kingdom of the Almighty, and all the children of flesh will call upon Thy name, when Thou wilt turn unto Thyself all the wicked of the earth. Let all the inhabitants of the world perceive and know that unto Thee every knee must bow, every tongue must swear.   Before

Thee, O Lord our God, let them bow and fall ; and unto Thy glorious name let them give honour ; let them all accept the yoke of Thy kingdom, and do Thou reign over them speedily, and for ever and ever. For the kingdom is Thine, and to all eternity Thou wilt reign in glory ; as it is written in Thy law, The Lord shall reign for ever and ever. And it is said, And the Lord shall be King over all the earth ; in that day shall the Lord be One, and His name One.'

But in spite of this prayer the general line of Rabbinic Judaism towards the ' nations ' was distinctly hostile and bitter. For, to the Jew, the Gentile was, on the whole, synonymous with the oppressor or the enemy. Israel alone knew God, and God was only 'near' to Israel.[1] But it seems fair to assert that Rabbinic Judaism, though it had a theory or two as to the reason why the one God who had undoubtedly 'created'

[1]Dr. Abrahams observes : ' This narrowness was softened by many human touches, for the Rabbinic particularism was never absolute, and several of its most prominent teachers spoke of the world outside Israel with love and fraternity. Rabbinism always held within itself the possibility of universalism, and this possibility was often realized in the doctrines and sympathies of the synagogue.'

all things and all men, was, nevertheless, in the best and most intimate sense, the divine Father of Israel only, or why Israel alone had the inestimable glory, privilege and happiness of practising the enactments of the perfect Law, did not greatly worry its head over the future lot of the Gentiles. It is true that even as late as 300 or 500 A.D. proselytes were by no means unknown. But the desire and the search for proselytes had ceased. When Christianity became the state church of the Roman Empire, it was forbidden under severe penalties for anybody to become a proselyte to Judaism. And even much earlier, after the Hadrianic war and its agonies, the tendency to shutting themselves off from the pitiless Gentile naturally tended to increase among the Jews. The distant future was for God. In the hard present let the Jew keep himself as much aloof as he could from the oppressor and the foe. The non-Jew was not a worshipper of the One God ; he was a sinner ; he was the enemy of Israel. After death he would undoubtedly receive (just as the Christian of 500 thought the Jew would receive) the reward of his unbelief and his wickedness. Meanwhile the Jew rejoiced in his own true and pure faith, and he thanked God for the special favour which the divine Father had vouchsafed to him. He thanked Him (as the prayer which immediately precedes the prayer already quoted, puts it) : ' that He has not made us like the nations of other lands, and has not placed us like other families of the earth, since He has not assigned unto us a portion as unto them, or a lot as unto all their multitude.' But what I am most keen to emphasize is that this indifference, dislike, contempt, particularism,—this ready and not unwilling consignment of the non-believer and the non-Jew to perdition and gloom,—was quite consistent with the most passionate religious faith and with the most exquisite and delicate charity. Just as heaps and heaps of Christians have devoutly believed that the unbeliever, or even the heretical Christian, would undoubtedly go to hell, and that he fully deserved to go there for his unbelief and

his sin, so was it *mutatis mutandis* with
the Jew.   And just as heaps and heaps of
these Christians, in spite of this odious particularism, lived noble lives, and loved God
with beautiful intensity, so was it also with
the Jews.   The odious particularism did not
affect their personal relations with God, or
their relations with their fellowmen within
the circle of their own community.   In fact
the particularism was usually more sub-
conscious than conscious.   As the ordinary
average Christian only consorted with
Christians, so the ordinary average Jew only
consorted with Jews.   The fate of the outsider did not thrust itself persistently within
the circle of his thought, and even when it
did, he could, such is the pathetic inconsistency of the human mind, consign the
outsider to perdition and truly love God at
one and the same time.   He could even
speak sincerely of a loving God, and really
believe in God's love, although he was convinced that a huge proportion of God's
children were born to an eternal 'death'!
Can there be a more perfect example of this

strange inconsistency than the author of the Fourth Gospel ?[1]

Now assume that I am right in my view of Rabbinic Judaism ; assume that the average and typical Rabbinic Jew of 300 or 500 was such as I have described. Picture him and his religion to yourself with their strength and their weakness ; their nobility and their limitations. And then ask yourself these questions : Is it conceivable that Paul before his conversion was such a Rabbinic Jew ? Is it conceivable that the religion of the man who had the vision at Damascus, and ultimately wrote the Epistle to the Romans, was, or had ever been, Rabbinic Judaism ? Whatever Paul's individual genius, whatever the effect of the conversion, whatever revolution the new faith wrought upon the materials of the old, is it conceivable that the one could have

---

[1]Dr. Abrahams remarks : ' It would be wrong to forget that long before the western world had heard of a " wider hope," Judaism, through the mouth-piece of its greatest medieval teacher, elevated into a dogma the second century saying of the Tosefta that " the pious of all nations have a share in the world to come." It is indeed on this pragmatic basis that Mendelssohn reared the structure of modern Judaism in its relation to the world.'

been built up even on the ruins of the other?

If Paul had previously only known and believed the markedly human view of the Messiah, would or could he have evolved his elaborate Christology ?

If he had concerned himself about the fate or the lot of the non-Jew as little as the typical Rabbinic Jew (of 500), would he have come to believe that his special mission was to the Gentiles ? (The question is justified even if we accept the theory that the consciousness of this special mission 'dawned on him only gradually,' that he first sought out, and attempted to convert, his own compatriots, and that it was his failure with these which stimulated his interest in the Gentiles, and turned his thoughts and activities in their direction.[1])

If he had held the Rabbinic view of the world, would he have acquired and taught his peculiar form of pessimism ?

If he had shared the Rabbinic view of the Law, could he conceivably have evolved the

[1]Dr. Vernon Bartlet in the article Paul—Encyc. Britt., 11th ed., p. 942, col. 1.—But weigh against this view the words of Loisy quoted in the Appendix.

particular theory about it elaborated in the Epistle to the Romans ?

If he had held the Rabbinic view of repentance, could he have ignored this conception so completely as he does ?

If his piety and communion with God had been purely of the Rabbinic type, could he have evolved his noble and peculiar mysticism ?

If his soteriology had been only that of Rabbinic Judaism, and he had known, and been attracted to, no other, could he have possibly devised and constructed the soteriology of the great Epistles ?

If his religious psychology had been that of Rabbinic Judaism, would it have been possible, even after Damascus, and after the conversion, for such a religious psychology to be evolved as we actually find (as much assumed as worked out) in the genuine writings of the Apostle ?

The two first questions are included for the sake of completeness, but raise no new point, and involve no difficulty. We know that after the rise and development of

Christianity, the more exalted and trans-
cendent views about the Messiah were aban-
doned by the Jews. A general reaction set
in. The other view that the Messiah would
be a mere man (however good), which had
been, so far as we can gather, the more
prevailing view of early Rabbinic Judaism,
gained ground : the ideas of pre-existence
and of semi-divinity, adopted by the
Apocalyptic thinkers and others both in
Palestine and in the Diaspora, became un-
popular, forgotten and taboo. Though to
Paul, Christ was not the Second Person of a
Trinity, though he was quite distinct from,
and subordinate to, the Divine Father, he
was nevertheless a regular divine being, who
had existed as divine before his incarnation,
and who, on his resurrection, was invested
with still greater power and glory than
before. He was God's own Son in a special
and peculiar sense. From the human
Messiah of the later Rabbinic Judaism he
was separated by an immense gulf. If Paul
had been a Rabbinic Jew of the 500 A.D.
type, he could hardly have made of the

human Jesus, who lived and died in Paul's own lifetime, what he actually made of him in the Epistles. Even if the Philippians and Colossians were not genuine, this conclusion would hold. The Christology of the Romans and Corinthians would have been difficult or impossible for such a Rabbinic Jew to achieve, however whole-heartedly he might have been converted to the belief that Jesus of Nazareth was the Messiah. But in the first half of the first century there was no such difficulty or impossibility.

As to the second question (concerning the fate or future of the Gentiles) we are aware that, even in Palestinian Judaism, there was, in the first century, a strong interest in proselytes and proselytism. In the Diaspora the interest was still greater. The facts are well-known and reported in detail in the text-books. A considerable fringe of persons existed who, without becoming full Jews, and accepting all the obligations of the Jewish Law, had nevertheless acknowledged the God of Israel as the one and only God, and offered worship to Him alone. Jewish

teachers were wont to lay stress upon the
moral, rather than the ritual, commands of
the Law, and if idolatry was forsworn, and
the simplest rules of morality observed, they
held and taught that such 'fearers of God'
would inherit the joys of the world to come.
We hear of a famous case in which a would-
be proselyte was told by a Jewish teacher
that he might even become a full Jew without submitting himself to circumcision.
These more liberal views still existed, even
after Hadrian.   One Rabbi declared that
the whole purpose of the dispersion of Israel
was that Gentile men and women might be
brought under the wings of the Shechinah.
Another went so far as to argue that
baptism would suffice for an adult male
proselyte without circumcision.   Hence
there is no reason why Paul, even before his
conversion, might not have been interested
in, or even troubled by, the religious condition and future of the Gentile world.   It
is just conceivable that he might have felt
that neither of the solutions offered so far
was perfectly satisfactory.   For it was

clearly very difficult for every Gentile to accept and follow out all the injunctions of the Law.   On the other hand, the ' outer fringe,' though their lot after death was secured, were nevertheless in *this* world put in a position of religious inferiority.   They had less obligations, but also less privileges. How then was the wall of separation between Jew and Gentile ever to be broken down ?   But if Paul did have any thoughts and reflections of this kind, they were probably suggested to him by a non-Jewish environment.   His noble religious universalism—his great doctrine of the absolute religious equality of Gentile and Jew—was probably led up to (as we shall see) by religious influences which lay outside the range of Rabbinic Judaism.

It is, however, the remaining six questions which constitute the real difficulty. Here is where the true problem lies.   It is in them that we find the full divergence between Rabbinic Judaism and Paul—that amazing divergence which has struck and puzzled those Jewish scholars who thought that they knew what Rabbinic Judaism really was (I admit that they are wont to take too purely favourable a view of it), and who reject (with perhaps excessive indignation) what they regard as the imaginary Rabbinic Judaism, created by Christian scholars, in order to form a suitably lurid background for the Epistles of St. Paul.

Now this immense divergence between Rabbinic Judaism and Paul does not mean that there was any decisive reason why, if Paul had been a typical Rabbinic Jew, he should not have become a Christian, that he should not have come to believe that Jesus of Nazareth was the predicted Messiah. It does not mean that there is any reason why he should not have taught that the Law was not binding on the Gentile believer, or even that, as the Messianic era was at hand, its observance was altogether unnecessary. It does not mean that there is any reason why he should not have attacked the various weaknesses and faults in Rabbinic Judaism, some of which, as we know, were the defects of its qualities, or even why

F

he should not have realised that the predictions of the prophets concerning the conversion and ingathering of the nations were at last to be realised and fulfilled. All this is conceivable. But what, if he had been a typical Rabbinic Jew, is far less conceivable is that he could have constructed the theory of the Law which we actually find in the Epistle to the Romans, that he would so wholly have ignored the Rabbinic doctrine of repentance, or that his soteriology and his mysticism would ever have come into being. For these phenomena Paul's individual genius and the conversion at Damascus do not suffice. Paul must have been less than a Rabbinic Jew, and more. To explain him are needed : (1) a Judaism which was other than Rabbinic ; (2) religious influences, conceptions and practises which were not Jewish at all.

In fact, the supposition that Paul before his conversion was a Rabbinic Jew in the ordinary sense of the word, led to a sort of *impasse*, a *cul de sac* from which no escape seemed possible. You could argue :

' No one who was a Rabbinic Jew could have written the great Epistles even twenty years after his conversion. Therefore the Epistles are forgeries.' Or you could say : ' The Epistles are undoubtedly genuine. Therefore they were written by one who twenty years before had been a Rabbinic Jew.' As the former deduction was even more impossible than the latter (for all the great scholars regarded forgery as wholly out of the question), nothing remained but to say that the epistles are an inexplicable mystery, a psychological and theological puzzle to which we have not yet succeeded in finding the key. I felt this puzzle in 1894, but found very little recognition of it among the great Christian scholars. In 1911, however, Professor Lake writes : "It must be admitted that it is very hard to believe that the Epistles could have been written by the Rabbinical Jew whom critical fancy has read back from the Talmud into the first century ; and if we accept the criticism which identified the Judaism of the first century with that of two centuries later, Van Manen's criticism is not only proper, but perhaps unanswerable."[1]

Thus Professor Lake shows in what direction the solution of the puzzle must lie. Either the Rabbinic Judaism of 50 was not the Rabbinic Judaism of 500 (or 300), or Paul at the time of his conversion was no pure Rabbinic Jew. Professor Lake truly says that we know comparatively little about the various parties, sects and tendencies in Judaism before the fall of the Temple. This cautious reminder of ignorance is intended to indicate that a full solution of the puzzle may never be attainable. To this I would assent. But the next remark of the Professor's is, I think inadequate. ' Many Jews, especially in the Diaspora, were of a liberal and ethnicizing disposition.' That statement may be perfectly true, but it will not carry us far. It is not that Paul's antecedent Judaism must

---

[1] The Earlier Epistles of St. Paul by Kirsopp Lake (1911), p. 426. Van Manen was the distinguished Dutch scholar, Prof. Lake's predecessor in the chair of New Testament exegesis at the University of Leiden, who denied the authenticity of *all* the Pauline Epistles.

have differed from Rabbinic Judaism in
being more liberal and ethnicizing, but it
must have differed from it in many important features and doctrines in regard to
which the terms ' liberal and ethnicizing ' to
not come in or apply.

Let us recur again to the six questions,
and see more precisely wherein the divergence between Paul and Rabbinic Judaism
actually consists.   First as to the Pauline
pessimism.   I have pointed out that to
average and typical Rabbinic Judaism the
world is good.   It is God's world.   How
different is the doctrine of Paul.   The world
is under the domination of demons and of
Satan.   Paul even goes so far as to call Satan
the god of this world, an expression which,
to the average Rabbinic Jew, would verge
upon blasphemy.   External nature is in a
bondage of corruption.   All creation groans
and travails in pain.   It has been subjected
to vanity by God Himself from Adam's
day till the appearance of Christ.   (How
little can we picture Paul smelling the rose
and thanking God for its fragrance.)   God's

wrath hangs heavy upon all the world, and especially upon man. It is a wrath so comprehensive and severe that only an amazing expedient and a terrific catastrophe can satisfy and appease it.

Combine this pessimism with the doctrine of the Law. The wrath of God and the wretchedness of man have not been lessened by the Law, holy though it be. Israel is no exception to the universal sinfulness and the universal misery. The Law has brought neither happiness nor virtue, and it was not intended to bring them. The Law was a curse. It evoked the knowledge of sin. It strengthened the desire to sin. By the works of the Law no man can win God's favour or be regarded by God as righteous. No one becomes righteous through the Law, if only because no man can fulfil the Law.

Here again the gulf between Rabbinic Judaism and Paul is gigantic. To the former, not merely is the world good, not merely ought we to enjoy ourselves in it, when circumstances permit, but in Israel, at all events, much happiness and much goodness exist, and both are conditioned and caused by the Law. The Law is the dearest and most glorious of blessings and of joys. Now it can be argued that in the case of a convert his whole view of the world is sometimes changed: what was white is now black; what was black is now white. But even this occasional phenomenon would not account for Paul. If he had said that the Law was altogether bad and undivine, his theory would be almost easier for a Rabbinic Jew to have constructed. But he asserts that the Law itself is good and holy, and yet that it was the strength of sin. Now there was indeed one Rabbinic theory that the Messiah would come when sin was at its worst. When calamity and iniquity were at their height, then, amidst such birth-travails, would Messiah be born. But the theory was never brought into relation with the Law. The Law was always the cause of goodness and the source of joy. If man sinned, it was in spite, and not in virtue, of the Law. To throw the blame for human sin upon the Law—the perfect, the adored, the delightful—would be like throwing the blame upon God. And however much sin there seemed to be in the world, a pious Rabbinic Jew was also conscious of some observance and some righteousness. Is it really conceivable that the Pauline theory of the Law could have been evolved by a man who had actually known the homely joys and spiritual fervours which the Law produced in every typical Rabbinic household? Could such a one have said of himself that he had been ' blameless ' as regards the Law, and yet have won from it no delight, no satisfaction, no peace? If he had been ' blameless ' in the Law, he would have argued: ' So far as I have sinned, it is my own fault. So far as I have done right and reaped the joy of doing right, it is due to the Law. So far as I have yielded to temptation, I deplore my weakness ; so far as I have overcome it, I thank God for the Law. For through the Law have I conquered.' That, if he had been a Rab-

binic Jew, would have been Paul's standpoint up to his conversion.   And if that *had*
been his standpoint, the theory of the Law
as we find it in the Epistle to the Romans
would scarcely have been a psychological
possibility, however intense his faith might
have become in the Messiahship of Jesus,
the Son of God.[1]

The systematic, and (within limits) the
consistent character of the Pauline teaching
is curiously unlike Rabbinic theology.   No
doubt the Rabbis taught that there was a
terrible amount of sin in the world and
even in Israel, but their views were so much
less hard and fast, so much less driven home
and pushed to their extremest consequences,
so much less theoretic and one-sided.   Paul
was a great and fiery genius, whose mind
was working under the influence of a tremendous religious upheaval.   This explains

---

[1] It is only fair to admit that there may be another explanation,
namely, that Paul knew the Rabbinic theory of the Law, but
that after his conversion, and after much controversy, he forgot
it, or ignored it, and so gradually formed his own new conception.   It is also not impossible, I admit, that a strange
genius like Paul might have gradually become discontented,
even though reared amid the happy environment of
Rabbinic Judaism.   But this view, though conceivable, seems
to me, unlikely.

a good deal, but it by no means explains
everything.   God's anger is often spoken
about by the Rabbis, but with them it is
much less systematic and persistent than
with Paul,—at any rate in Israel. Throughout history and experience, it was, as they
believed, constantly crossed by His forgiveness, His compassion, His love. Of these we
hear very little in Paul, except in so far as
God's love was ultimately manifested, when
the tale of human sin and misery had
reached its culmination, by the death of
Christ with its far-reaching effects for salvation and for good. But for Rabbinic
theology (as for Jesus himself) God was so
good and near and kind, and man, through
the Law and through repentance, had such
constant, easy and efficacious opportunities
of access to Him, that there was no need of
a tremendous cosmic and divine event such
as was provided by the incarnation and the
crucifixion.   Things were by no means
so bad as Paul, in his pessimism, supposed.
There was some righteousness and happiness in the world, as well as much misery

and sin.   And even from sin and misery
there was a way out.   That way was constructed by God's forgiveness and man's
repentance.   Its outward symbol was the
Day of Atonement.   What neither God nor
man could do according to Paul except by
the incarnation of the Son, was done according to Rabbinic Judaism constantly,
hour by hour, and year by year.   Nothing
is more peculiar in the great Epistles than
the almost complete omission of the twin
Rabbinic ideas of repentance and forgiveness.   The very word for repentance is only
found in three passages.   The first of these
is in the second chapter of the Romans—a
chapter which has so many peculiar features
that do not easily fit in with the subsequent
teaching that Lietzmann declares that its
reasoning depends throughout upon an
hypothesis which (to the writer) is fictitious.
The other two passages are in the seventh
chapter of the second Epistle to the Corinthians, and here repentance is only spoken
of in connection with persons who already
were Christians, and had nevertheless sinned.

The same is the case in regard to the single occasion in which the verb ' repent ' is employed by Paul (2 Cor. xii. 21).[1]

This strange and fundamental difference between Pauline and Rabbinic theology seems scarcely conceivable if Paul up to his conversion had been a typical Rabbinic Jew. At least one might have expected that, in his allusions to the Jews, Paul would somewhere have said : ' your repentance, about which you talk so much, is not adequate, and God's forgiveness, of which you prate so constantly, will not be extended to you.' The Jews would doubtless have refused to believe him, but at any rate he would not have ignored the very keynote of their whole position.[2]

---

[1] A learned friend observes : ' I think you lay too much stress on the rarity of the mere words. True, the words are rare, but in every mention of the Cross, the thought is there, and if ever there was a man who felt he was forgiven, it was Paul. I feel sure that the sense of forgiveness coloured his whole thought, however rarely expressed.' My friend's objection partly confirms my view. Undoubtedly the sense of forgiveness coloured his whole *Christian* thought just because it had been absent from his *Jewish* thought. If he had been a Rabbinic Jew, with the words and the thoughts of repentance and forgiveness constantly on his lips and in his heart, he would not have needed to establish the theory of the Cross.

[2] I admit that one must always remember that the Epistles are controversial letters rather than theological doctrines,

For these reasons the Pauline soteriology seems to me impossible upon a purely Rabbinic basis. The origin of the hard opposition between ' faith ' and ' works ' will always remain something of a puzzle. But it is much more a puzzle (so far as its development in the apostle's mind is concerned) if we think of him up till his conversion as a typical Rabbinic Jew. The excellence of faith was not unknown to, or uncelebrated by, Rabbinic Judaism, but it was never opposed to works.[1] If one had faith in God, one naturally tried to fulfil his commands. Faith and works were parts of a single whole. According to Rabbinic theology, God could and did carry out the whole process of salvation Himself. There was no need of a Son, for nothing was left for him to do. Salvation was the privilege of every Israelite who, believing in God and in His Law, tried to do his best,

---

and that Paul is dealing primarily with Jewish Christians rather than with Jews.

[1] 'Ce n'est pas dans la tête d'un Juif palestinien qu'aurait pu germer la pensée d'une antinomie entre la foi et la loi—aussi bien Jésus n'en a-t-il pas même le soupçon.' Loisy in Revue d'histoire et de littérature religieuses, vol. iv., p. 490 (1913).

and was sorry for his failures and his lapses. I do not think that to the Rabbinic Jew sin was less hateful than it was to Paul, but he objectified it less ; moreover, he thought that God's power was greater and that sin's power was less. Therefore it was unnecessary that a sinless divine being should ' become sin ' on man's behalf. Man could receive salvation, and get the better of sin, (for God was always helping and forgiving) even without so strange and wonderful a device.

Rabbinic theology had no elaborate theory about the relative functions of God and man in human goodness. It spoke freely about God's help : in Rabbinic prayers that help is frequently implored ; but at the same time it is not supposed that human efforts count for nothing. Virtue and vice have a meaning : goodness and badness are real. They would have no such true significance if man were not *really* to blame when he sinned, and *really* to be praised when he succeeded and did well. Man co-operates with God. His will is free.

He can choose the good or the evil. And
though he often chooses the evil, he also
often chooses the good. It is not that the
Rabbis were conceited or self-righteous. It
is that they looked on facts as they were,
and saw life as it was. They neither de-
preciated human goodness on the one hand,
nor over-estimated it on the other. And,
above all, they were not theorists, and had
little philosophy. They spoke of flesh and
of spirit : they knew of the baser desires of
the body, and how human sin was connected
with human flesh. They believed that God
was spirit and not flesh. But they did not
oppose flesh and spirit in the same way as
they are opposed in the writings of Paul ;
and, above all, they did not make a distinction between the spiritual man on the one
hand, and the merely psychic (or 'natural')
man upon the other. Here most decidedly
we touch un-Rabbinic ground. Rabbinic
theory did not hold that man could only
conquer and free himself from sin if he was
born again and regenerated by the divine
spirit ; it taught a less antithetical doc-

trine, and admitted more shades and degrees. It did not divide people off into ' those in the flesh,' who cannot do good, and ' those in the spirit ' who (theoretically) cannot do evil. The spirit and flesh doctrine of the eighth chapter of the Epistle to the Romans could not have been devised by anyone who, to his Rabbinic antecedents, merely added a conviction that the Messiah had appeared in the person of Jesus. The man who devised that doctrine had not only been subjected to other influences, but he had never been thoroughly imbued with true Rabbinical theology. It was not bone of his bone, or else the new teaching could not have been conceived and thought out. There would have been no need of it ; no adequate impulse to set it going.[1]

---

[1] In all these matters the view of the Rabbis was the view of Jesus. What Piepenbring says, for instance, of Jesus in contrast to Paul is absolutely true of the Rabbis in contrast to Paul. For example, " Se plaçant uniquement sur le terrain pratique, il se contentait, à l'instar des grands prophètes, de prêcher la repentance et l'accomplissement fidèle de la volonté de Dieu, comme seuls moyens de salut, en supposant toujours l'homme capable d'y suffire par ses propres forces. Voilà pourquoi il ne dit jamais que celui-ci a besoin d'être éclairé ou régénéré par le Saint Esprit ou d'être transformé en homme nouveau par la foi, par les sacraments ou par un autre moyen quelconque." (*Jésus et les Apôtres*, p. 214.)

So far, then, we have seen that the religion of Paul antecedent to his conversion must have been different from the typical and average Rabbinic Judaism of 300 or 500, but not in that difference more ' liberal and ethnicizing.' The curious, and, I fancy, novel conclusion seems imperative that (in the matters just gone through) it was a religion poorer than, and even inferior to, the typical and average Rabbinic Judaism of 300 or 500. It may have been more systematic, and perhaps a little more philosophic and less child-like, but possibly for these very reasons it was less intimate, warm, joyous and comforting. Its God was more distant and less loving. He was less immediately concerned with Israel and with the world ; He left more ' spheres of influence ' to the control of angels and devils. The early religion of Paul was more sombre and gloomy than Rabbinic Judaism ; the world was a more miserable and God-forsaken place ; there were fewer simple joys and happinesses which could and should be sanctified by religion, and then temperately

G

enjoyed.   The outlook was darker : man could be, and was, less good ; his actions were looked at with a jaundiced eye.   Man repented less, and less successfully ; God was not constantly helping and forgiving. It needed the poverty and the pessimism of the Pauline pre-Christian Judaism to have produced the Pauline Christianity.   From the Rabbinic Judaism of 500 as basis, many salient doctrines of the great Epistles could never have been evolved.   They would have been so very unnecessary, and, because unnecessary, they could not have been thought out.

These arguments apply, I think, to five of my eight questions.   For the Christology and the universalism other considerations (as we have already seen) come into play. Both the one and the other may, to some extent, be accounted for by well-known features of Jewish thought in the first century, though the universalism probably also needed the stimulus of external and non-Jewish influences.

The same may be said of the noble Pauline

mysticism.   That mysticism depends upon
the death and resurrection of the divine
being, Jesus Christ.   It is expressed in a
spiritual imitation of that death which will
lead up to a union with the Risen One in
glory.   But the imitated death, and the new
life which it brings, are mystically undergone here and now.   The union is so complete that the old personality has vanished;
it is Christ who lives within the soul.   The
man who is in Christ is a new creature ;
the old man is crucified with Christ ; the
sinful body is destroyed.   The Christian
is buried with Christ through the baptism
of death, so that, as Christ was raised
from the dead through the glory of the
Father, the Christian may walk even on
earth in a new life.   He, the Christian, is
no longer in the flesh, but in the Spirit.
It is the Spirit which is his true life even
on earth ; it is the Spirit of Christ, which
is the Spirit of God, that will give him,
and him alone, the life of the resurrection.
Dying with Christ is dying to sin.   It is
the sudden production of a new and higher

existence, which is not interrupted, but glorified, by death. For the Spirit, which has virtually annulled this body of sin, will then be given the spiritual body that befits it. In this new and higher existence, endowed with the Spirit, the new man possesses, at last, the power to sin no more. He can will the good and accomplish it. The Spirit needs no written and external law : the Spirit, which is Christ, fulfils its own law, the law of Christ, the law of faith, the law of love.

This striking, enthusiastic, inspiring mysticism, which has impelled to many noble deeds of sacrifice and of love, could hardly have grown up from a purely Jewish soil. So far as it was not created by Paul sheerly and merely on the basis of his conversion, experience and genius, we must look for its genesis outside Rabbinic Judaism whether of 300 or of 30, of 500 or of 50. To Rabbinic Judaism God was near. The thought of Him, the service of Him, was a perpetual joy. But just as the higher life with God was not brought about by any magical sacrament, so it was not realised by any mystic process or mystic faith. The Rabbinic Jew did not seek to become one with God; he knew, but made little use of, the idea of dying to live; he did not think of God as in him or of himself as in God. There might be sudden repentance and complete forgiveness, but conceptions such as those of a new creation, a spiritual re-birth, an attainment or a bestowal of the divine Spirit, an inward illumination, a flooding of the soul with light, though not wholly unknown, were no regular part of his system and very seldom before his mind. His religious life did not move on *lower* lines; it moved upon *different* lines. He did not love God less: he loved Him in another way.

If then Paul's pre-Christian religion was not Rabbinic Judaism as we know it, what does this imply? It might imply (among other things) that Rabbinic Judaism as we know it—the Rabbinic Judaism of 300, 400 or 500 A.D. had not come into being in 50. Was the most un-Hellenistic, most

purely Palestinian, Rabbinic Judaism of
50, a poorer, colder, gloomier religion than
its descendant of 300, 400 and 500 ?   And
now being once more brought face to face
with this difficult and delicate question,
without possibility of further postponement
or evasion, I must honestly declare that it is
not for me to answer, or attempt to answer
it !   I must leave it to the great scholars.
Let men such as Abrahams or Buechler,
Bacher or Schechter, instruct us.[1] For the
question is surely an intensely interesting
one, and we would like to hear the answer,
so far as an answer is possible.[2]   One point
seems clear. It has been made before, but it
bears constant repetition. So far as the
Rabbinic Judaism of 500 was richer, warmer,

---

[1] Since these words were written, Professor Bacher, perhaps
the greatest of the four, has passed away.

[2] Dr. Abrahams tells me that, so far as he is concerned, he
believes that there was no great upheaval as a result of the
destruction of the Temple in 70, but that, on the contrary,
there are to be detected the same general qualities in the
Rabbinic Judaism as expressed in the teaching and life of
Hillel—at the beginning of the Christian era—of Jochanan
ben Zakkai—at about the period of the Temple's fall—and of
Akiba—at the period of complete loss of the national independence (135 A.D.) He believes, moreover (and this is the crucial
point), that these same general qualities are found in the
Rabbinic Judaism of the entire Talmudic period.

more joyous, and more optimistic than the
Rabbinic Judaism of 50, it was not all this
because it was less legal. For legalism and
the love of the Law were not *less* prevailing
and universal in 500 than they were in 50 :
they were more. The empire and domination of the Law were more complete and
pervasive than ever ; so that the Pauline
theories of the Law, which probably did not
fit the facts of Rabbinic Jewish life in 50,
most undoubtedly missed them in 500.
Whatever may have been the case in 50,
in 500 the Law brought peace and joy and
life : it produced righteousness and evoked
love : it made men realise, and brought
them near unto, God.

I am, however, inclined to think that,
even in 50, Rabbinic Judaism was a better,
happier, and more noble religion than one
might infer from the writings of the Apostle.
There are no signs of any great improvement
in the teachings of the famous Rabbis of the
fourth century over those of the first. There
is no violent break between the character
of the Rabbinic teaching (so far as we can

gather it) before and after the fall of the Temple. It is true that the shock of the destruction of state and temple, and the awful catastrophe of the Hadrianic war, tended to a certain amount of pessimism, but even in the worst times we hear of the gloom of one Rabbi being cheered by the optimism of another, and there is little reason to believe that before the Temple fell any large measure of pessimism (such as we have inferred for the pre-Christian religion of the Apostle) existed at all. In one point only was the Rabbinic Judaism of the first century probably much inferior to the Rabbinic Judaism of the fourth or fifth. In the first century the opposition between the learned and the ignorant must have been much more intense and more violent than it afterwards became. A class of people existed who, for one reason or another, did not observe the Law, and were regarded by the teachers as outcasts and reprobates. But it is an interesting fact that these people, who form a back ground for the life and teaching of Jesus, do not do so for Paul.

Whatever Paul's religion may have been before his conversion, he was never (so far as we know) a member of the ' outcast,' or ignorant class.   He does not concern himself with those who were really outside the legal pale.   He does not come forward with a message for the ' sinners,' that is, for those regarded as ' sinners ' by the ' righteous ' legalists.   It is the legalists themselves whom he declared to be on the wrong track, and it is the ' righteousness ' of the Law which he attacks.   Hence this particular weakness of the Rabbinic Judaism of the first century, while it explains a good deal in Jesus, does not explain Paul.   It is indeed possible that in one particular department of life the Law may have been more burdensome in the first century than it afterwards became.   It is possible that the enactments about ritual purity, which we know to have caused little bother or trouble to the ordinary layman in the fourth or fifth century, may have caused more bother and trouble to the layman of the first century before the Temple fell.   The subject is complicated and disputed. But even if, in this one respect, the observance of the Law in the first century was more burdensome than it subsequently became, I still venture to believe that Paul's Judaism was tolerably far removed from contemporary Rabbinic Judaism, even allowing for the possibility that the Rabbinic Judaism of 50 was of a somewhat poorer religious quality than the Rabbinic Judaism of 500. I am, therefore, disposed to look with much suspicion upon the statement in the Acts, and none the less because it is put into the mouth of the Apostle, that Paul 'was brought up in Jerusalem, at the feet of Gamaliel, instructed according to the strict manner of the law of our fathers.'[1]   Professor Lake,

---

[1] ' Tout ce que racontent les Actes au sujet de Paul avant sa conversion est grandement suspect. Ce qui est dit là de Gamaliel serait beaucoup plus certain si on le trouvait dans une Épitre de Paul, mais c'est dans un discours des Actes, conséquemment dans une composition du rédacteur, et la mention de Gamaliel (déjà mentionné, Act v. 34-39, passage de couleur légendaíre) n'offre pas plus de garanties d'historicité que la participation de Paul au meurtre d'Étienne. Si ces indications étaient vraies, Paul aurait dû être à Jerusalem quand Jésus y vint, et il aurait assisté également à la naissance de la première communauté. Or les Épitres ne laissent entendre rien de semblable. . . . . Bien qu'il vante son orthodoxie, Paul n'a jamais été qu'un pharisien de province, un juif de la dispersion.' From M. Loisy's reviews of Böhlig,

who wants and likes to accept as much of Acts as he can, avoids the trouble of this statement in a clever and humorous way. He says, ' Saul of Tarsus may have been a pupil of Gamaliel, and been profoundly affected by him, and yet may have succumbed to other influences. We do not always follow all the opinions of our teachers, and it would be scarcely suggested that our books are not authentic because they do not agree with the teaching which we received at our Universities or Theological Colleges.'[1] It may, however, be doubted whether this ingenious explanation is adequate. In any case we have to consider that in the sense in which we can speak of Rabbinic Judaism in 300 or 500, and probably in the sense in which we can speak of Rabbinic Judaism in 50 or 30, Paul was no Rabbinic Jew.

Die Geisteskultur von Tarsos im augusteischen Zeitalter, in his own Revue d'histoire et de littérature religieuses (vol. iv. 1913, p. 490), and in the Revue critique (1913) No. 30, p. 64. Böhlig (p. 111) rightly says : " Nicht Jerusalem, sondern Tarsos und überhaupt die Diaspora ist die Heimstätte der jüdischen Gedanken Pauli. Seine Zugehörigkeit zur Jüngerschaft Gamaliel's war nur eine Episode in seinem Leben.'

[1] Earlier Epistles of Paul, p. 427.

What sort of a Jew was he then ? Here
it may seem that I have been flogging a
dead horse. For everybody admits that
Paul was a Jew of the Diaspora, or, putting
it more precisely, that he was an Hellenistic
Jew. And his Christology and his intense
belief in the nearness of the Messianic age
show, in all probability, that, even before
his conversion, he had been influenced by
the Apocalyptic school of thinkers or
dreamers, many of whom held advanced
views about the nature of the Messiah, and
all of whom were inclined to believe that the
longed-for end was at hand. The elements,
however, in his doctrine which have led
many scholars to discuss the degree to which
he was influenced by his Hellenistic environment, or again the features in his
teaching which link him up with some of the
Apocalyptic seers, did not prevent these
scholars from describing his Jewish background as Rabbinic. They made, perhaps,
an exception for certain aspects of his
doctrine which seemed to prove that, together with a devotion to the Law, he also

united certain 'liberal and ethnicizing' features which were anything but Rabbinic. I go further. My point is that the very spirit of Paul's pre-Christian religion, quite apart from any possible liberal and ethnicizing tendencies, was other than the spirit of Rabbinic Judaism. It was different from the Rabbinic Judaism of 300 or 500, and it was in all probability other than the Rabbinic Judaism of 50 or 30. It was other than Rabbinic Judaism because it was colder, less intimate, less happy, because it was poorer, more pessimistic. And I am inclined to believe that it was all this—that it possessed these inferiorities —just because it was not Rabbinic Judaism, but Diaspora Judaism. I am inclined to believe that so far from Diaspora Judaism being greatly superior to Rabbinic Judaism, it was often (not always) inferior, and that the pre-Christian religion of Paul tended towards this poorer and inferior type. And thus my thesis is the reverse of the usual thesis. The usual thesis, I think, is that, so far as Paul is to be explained by having been an Hellenistic Jew, this means that he had a better religion than if he had been a pure Rabbinic Jew. My thesis, on the contrary, is that so far as Paul was an Hellenistic Jew, and so far as that fact can explain him, he had not a better religion than Rabbinic Judaism, but a religion colder and more sombre.

A Hellenistic Jew could be, and usually was, a ' legal ' Jew. He too could describe himself ' as touching the Law a Pharisee ' (though all this passage in the Philippians has, it must be admitted, no genuine Jewish ring), or again as one who had ' advanced in the Jews' religion beyond many of his own age among his countrymen, being more exceedingly jealous for the traditions of his fathers.' He could fancy himself perfectly orthodox. But, for all that, his religion was frequently not in all respects the religion of Rabbinic Jews. It often seems to have differed from it in those very points which constitute the essence and bloom of a religion, different less in dogma than in attitude, less in creed than in outlook and in emotion.

The God of many Hellenistic and Apocalyptic Jews seems to me to have been a less intimate, near and affectionate God than the God of Rabbinic Judaism. A small contact with philosophy seems to have made God more distant and less approachable. The God of the Rabbis was very personal and childlike ; He did not care for system and theories ; but, at all events, He was always there when wanted, and He managed His own affairs Himself. He loved and was loved. The grandiose conceptions of the Apocalyptic seers, and the influence of Greek philosophy, made Him more august and majestic, but less gentle and kindly. Thus arose the greater necessity for intermediaries between God and man—angels, messiahs, or sons. The Rabbinic God dealt directly with His human children, and forgave them without intercessor or middleman.

Hellenistic and Apocalyptic Judaism, so far as the latter can be safely distinguished as a separate type, strike us, when we read their literary products, as less human and childlike than Rabbinic Judaism, and as more sombre and austere. The fourth book of Ezra was written not long after the destruction of the Temple, when all Jews, whether Rabbinic, Apocalyptic, or Hellenistic, were inclined to be sorrowful and gloomy. Nevertheless the fact remains that in its pessimism and despair it offers the most striking contrast to the extant Rabbinic writings. Rabbinic Judaism, just because of its essentially happy faith, had the power to recover from the shock of the Temple's fall, and even from the still more appalling agony of the Hadrianic revolt. Rabbinic Judaism not only recovered, but became, or, as I am inclined to believe, became again, a human and joyous religion, declaring that, in spite of all which had happened, the world was God's world still.

Hellenistic Judaism was, I suppose, more on the defensive than Rabbinic Judaism. It had to look outwards rather than inwards, and began to invent theories and justifications of its religion instead of accepting it as a delightful matter of course. May we not also suppose that the general spiritual anxiety which was widely diffused in the later Hellenistic world had also infected the Jews ? Some of them, too, may have begun to worry about their salvation and the ' state of their soul.' And as God had become more distant, so did sin seem, not more grievous, but less eradicable, than to their ' Rabbinic ' brethren. Human repentance and divine forgiveness were ideas never far from the Rabbinic mind : we hear less of them from the Hellenists. God helps less and forgives less ; man continues more persistently in sin. The Hellenistic Jew was more theoretic and systematic, but his outlook on life was less accurate and less sensible.

Why the Day of Atonement should have played a less potent part in Jewish Hellenistic life I do not clearly understand, but it seems probable that it must have done so.[1]

---

[1] A learned friend observes : ' Was it not because human nature rebels against the sense of sinfulness and the creed of

H

However closely and ardently the Hellenistic Jew clung to the Law, it meant something different to him from what it meant to his full-fledged Rabbinic brother. Greeks and barbarians laughed at some of the ceremonial enactments, and did not the Jew begin to wonder why such queer injunctions had been ordained ?   We know that Philo could only approve of, and admire, some of the Pentateuchal commandments because of the inner spiritual meaning which they were supposed to contain, while an extreme radical wing of Jewish Hellenists at Alexandria adopted these inner meanings, and (to Philo's indignation) neglected the outward observance.

To the Jew of the Diaspora who was disposed to take a gloomy view of the universal domination of sin, might not the wonder occasionally arise (as indeed it did arise to the author of the fourth book of Ezra) how it was that the Law, given by God for Israel's welfare, had yet not been

atonement, and that that sense rises or falls with the environment ? Hellenism knows nothing of it.' If so, it is another instance of the subtle influence of environment.

able to destroy the evil impulse and the wicked heart ? The more commandments, the more opportunities for transgression. Yet the Law had to be tenaciously and consciously clung to and justified. The Rabbinic Jew did not need to justify the most adorable of God's gifts, the most joyous of the Israelite's possessions. He took it at its own valuation, and loved it for its own sake. Directly you have to justify a thing, it becomes a little external ; you hold it at arm's length, and examine it curiously. If you live with it, and grow with it, and accept it as a matter of course, you love it without asking why, and it becomes a part of your own very self. You do not compare it with anything else. It is just your own, a sheer privilege and delight. Perhaps the Hellenistic Jew was too much surrounded by other people to feel like that about the Law. Again, *within* the community the negative injunctions of the Law on the ceremonial side were hardly felt at all. Who bothers his head to-day that he is not given for his food the flesh of dogs and cats and horses ? The Rabbinic Jew, in the recesses of his own community, had no special desire to eat pig or rabbit or hare ; while he ate his mutton, he did not long to drink some milk. But the Hellenistic Jew began to worry himself as to the meaning and value of these enactments : he ate no hares, but many a Gentile neighbour, whose language he shared, ate hares and rabbits too, and laughed at the Jew because he refused to eat them. Did then the Law become to him rather a series of Do not's than a series of Do's ? Did he think of it more in its negative than in its positive aspects ? If so, unlike the Rabbinic Jew, he would think of it as something which restrained and forbade, rather than as something through which he gained ineffable joys and realised the presence of God.

The religious views of Paul *after* his conversion appear to me an inexplicable psychological enigma unless we assume that, *before* his conversion, his religion was less intimate and joyous than Rabbinic Judaism, on the one hand, and more theoretic and questioning, upon the other. In spite (partly perhaps as a cause) of his fanaticism, he must have had his anxieties and perhaps even his doubts. He must have had his worries both about his own salvation and about the salvation of his fellows. Repentance and forgiveness had receded into the background. The very Law which he defended had its difficulties and its puzzles.

We have seen that the joy of the commandments,—that simple happiness in performing any particular injunction of the Law —seems to be a special and peculiar feature of Rabbinic Judaism. I have myself no doubt that it already existed in 50, though it was perhaps more widespread in 500. But if already known in Jerusalem, it had, we may suppose, not yet penetrated to Tarsus. On the other hand, the supposed burden of the Law does not seem to have affected the Apostle very greatly. The attack of Matthew xxiii. 4, upon the Scribes and Pharisees (' they bind heavy burdens,' etc.) is not repeated in the Epistles. Nor do we hear anything as to the 'endless details,' the 'innumerable ceremonial minutiæ,' the 'arbitrary and trivial commands,' not 'lit up by any single principle,' with which the text-books have made us familiar.

(The 'elements' of Colossians and Galatians, even though 'weak and beggarly,' do not precisely imply a 'bondage' of this kind.) The Law was to Paul a whole, and it is curious how very rarely he separates (as Jesus seems to do) its ceremonial from its moral enactments. His main points are, first, that if you are under the Law, you must observe it altogether and, secondly, that failure is inevitable. But the famous passage in the seventh chapter of the Romans must be used with a little caution as an indication of Paul's individual experience before his conversion.[1] In any case the theory there elaborated does not depend upon the ceremonial enactments of the Pentateuch. If there were nothing in the Pentateuch but moral laws, and of these

---

[1] Brückner—Die Entstehung der paulinischen Christologie, p.220 (1903). Loisy in Revue d'histoire et de littérature religieuses. Vol. iii., 1912, p. 572 *ad init.*

not more than half a dozen, the argument of the seventh chapter would still hold good. And though Paul, as I believe, had undoubtedly pondered before his conversion upon the deep ingrained sinfulness of man and the difficulty of right-doing, the argument in the Romans is not so much based upon personal experience as it is a general deduction from, and a summing-up of, the full-blown theory of sin and law as he had constructed it *after* his conversion. The person who speaks is not so much Paul as humanity as a whole. But no Rabbinic Jew could ever have accepted the force, or the argument, of that seventh chapter. For it was precisely the Law which to his mind enabled him and all others to attain to any measure of human goodness. Without the Law they would be in bondage and in the darkness of sin ; through the Law they reached up to freedom, to righteousness and to God. ' There is no liberty except in the Torah.' So enormous is the gulf which separates the religion of Paul from the religion of any noble Rabbinic Jew, and yet both of them were filled with the spirit of God.   But if Paul before his conversion had been a thorough Rabbinic Jew, the seventh chapter of the Romans could scarcely have been written.

Paul's doctrine of the Law is remarkable both for what it says and what it omits. One could have imagined that he might have argued thus : 'Jesus Christ is Messiah, and the end of the present world is at hand. Moreover in Jesus Christ the barrier between Jew and Gentile has been broken down. There is no longer need of, or propriety in, separative ceremonial enactments.   The Law had only to be observed till Jesus came and lived and died and rose.[1]   Now neither Jewish nor Gentile Christian need observe it any longer.[2]   For now all that is neces-

---

[1] We may here recall the Rabbinic theory (the date of which is, however, uncertain), that the ceremonial laws were no longer to be observed in the Messianic age.

[2] I am well aware that the great name of Harnack can be cited against the truth of the assertions in this sentence. Harnack writes to vindicate the Lucan authorship and the historic accuracy of the whole book of Acts.   There is no grave inconsistency between the Paul of the Letters and the Paul of Acts.   I venture to think that Harnack has not proved his case.   Two excellent articles against his inter- pretation of certain passages in the Epistles, which would appear to militate against what I have said in the text, are

sary is a warm and living faith in
Jesus Christ, and with this faith all men
will receive the spirit of God, and will
obtain the force to enable them to do the
right. The separating ceremonial laws
have become otiose, for all men are one in
Christ ; the moral laws will be obeyed
because of the possession of the spirit.
Faith in Jesus Christ is all that is necessary
in order to carry the believer onward into
the new era which cannot be far off. And
even if that new era be delayed, even so,
faith is adequate for righteousness. It
justified Abraham in the eyes of God. It
will justify the believer now. It will justify
him in the sense of freeing him from the
divine wrath ; it will justify him also in
the sense of destroying his sinful nature,
giving him a new nature, making him a new
man.' Again, we should not have been surprised had Paul attacked the many accre-
tions of the Oral Law, had he spoken of the

those of P. W. Schmiedel, ' Galater v. 3, in neuester Aus-
legung ' (in the Protestantische Monatshefte, 1911, p. 318—
322), and A. Jülicher, ' Die jüdischen Schranken des Harnack-
schen Paulus' (in same magazine, 1913, p. 1-20.) Cp. also
E. Vischer in Theologische Rundschau, 1913, p. 256-258.

dangers of legalism in promoting self-righteousness and hypocrisy.

But though these lines of argument and these criticisms are not wholly wanting in the Epistles, they are not by any means predominant. The important thing is that Paul does not content himself with saying that the Law was all very well, and did very well, up to Jesus Christ's day, but need not now, (and, therefore, should not now), be observed any more, but that he actually conceived the theory that the Law did definite and positive harm. It was not all very well, and did not do all very well, up to Jesus, but it was all very bad, and did exceedingly ill.[1] It was not a blessing, and the source of life, and a freedom, and a joy, and the means of righteousness, as the Jews supposed and said, up to Jesus, and it was not merely *now* these things no more, but it had *never been* any one of them from the day of its bestowal, and, what is more, it had never been *intended* to be any of them. It

---

[1] A learned friend observes : ' Note how Luke puts into Peter's mouth the amazing statement, Acts xv. 10. This seems like Paulinism at the gallop.'

made things worse than they were, or than they would have been, without it. And all this was its intention, the purpose for which it had been given. The worst sinners were the sinners of Israel (Paul does not actually say this, but it seems to follow from his argument), and to produce this excess and heightened quality of sin was just the very object of the Law ! The supernatural and divine redemption was intended to overcome and conquer sin at its very height of quality and of amount. That Jesus Christ might bring freedom and sonship, the Law was to cause an acute servitude and a conscious bondage.[1]

The heat of antagonism may well have carried Paul from point to point in his strictures upon the Law, but even making all allowance for that antagonism, I cannot

---

[1] Dr. Abrahams observes : ' Rabbinic Judaism held, it is true, that the Israelite sinner was the more culpable because he disobeyed a law binding on Jews, than he would have been had he sinned with no law to obey. But the meaning was that to sin against the light is worse morally than to sin when no guiding light is present. This is quite different from the Pauline theory that the Law created sin. On the contrary, the Law imparted the power to recognise sin and resist it. The Law was the test and the antidote, the diagnosis and the remedy.''

believe that this absolute *bouleversement*, this complete topsy-turvydom, of the Rabbinic position could ever have been reached if that Rabbinic position had once been his own faith. Even the theory that sin was to be at its height when Messiah appeared cannot account for it satisfactorily. If Paul, like an ordinary Rabbinic Jew, had habitually thought of God as the divine Father, and of the Israelites as His human sons and children, if he had habitually thought of the Law as the source of freedom and of holiness, I do not think that any amount of controversy and mutual hatred could ever have produced the Epistle to the Galatians. But the heat and bitterness of antagonism might well have sufficed to produce it, if Paul's pre-Christian religion had been that poorer, more distant and more pessimistic type of Judaism such as I have attempted to describe. And to this pessimism as regards man's actual, psychological endowment, and as regards his inveterate tendency to sin, may be added what Paul read in the Scriptures, how the Law had historically failed to keep the Israelite from constant apostasy and evil-doing, and how, according to the too general dogma both of the Biblical writers and of his own time, all the weary and continued misfortunes and troubles of his fellow believers were due to their never-ending transgressions and iniquities. To these general explanations may be added the unbelief of the great majority of the Jews in the Messiahship of Jesus and in the Gospel. The unbelief was wilful: the light, the teaching, the salvation, were presented to them, and consciously and deliberately were they refused. In that age only one deduction was possible: all the unbelieving Jews were sinners. For the idea and the conviction that a man can be a wilful unbeliever and yet morally virtuous is purely modern.[1] Just as the Jews more and more

---

[1] Even so great, and, in many ways, so tolerant a man as Erasmus, when thoroughly irritated and depressed by the conflict with Luther, can write the amazing words : ' Deterior enim est, qui recedit ab ecclesiæ consortio et in hæresim aut schisma demigrat, quam qui impure vivit salvis dogmatibus.' (Völker, Toleranz und Intoleranz im Zeitalter der Reformation, 1912, p. 188.)

tended to suppose that those who accepted Jesus as the Messiah were of necessity wicked, so Paul was bound to suppose that those who rejected his Messiahship were necessarily depraved and sinful. But if they clung to their Law and were sinful, was not the next step to argue that the tighter they clung the more they sinned, and that the Law, of which they boasted so outrageously, was the very source and cause of their sin ?

Nor was the Law without its puzzles as regards the Gentiles. If Rabbinic Judaism had an occasional qualm about the darkness of the heathen world, if it had to invent an occasional theory to account for the religion and the joys of the Law having been vouchsafed to so small a fraction of the human race (while nevertheless God was the ruler and creator of all), we may safely surmise that such qualms and theories were more frequent in the Hellenistic communities. The author of the 4th book of Ezra gives up the whole question of the heathen as an impossibly hopeless puzzle.

' Touching man in general, Thou knowest best, but touching Thy people I will speak !' The Apocalyptic seers were accustomed to consign thousands with equanimity to perdition, and on the orthodox side the author of the 4th book of Ezra tries to urge with odious emphasis that it was quite the proper thing for this world to be for many, and for the next world to be for few. Even so God was compassionate ! Few would be the saved of Israel ; still fewer, if any, the saved of the Gentiles. But like the author of the 4th book of Ezra in his better moments of recoil and question, some other Apocalyptic, and some Hellenistic, Jews may have had compunctions over this immensity of ruin. Paul, as we know, could bear strong meat in more senses than one. And he too could send unbelievers to destruction without shrinking or pity. But even before his conversion may he not have had his troubles about the reason why God had created so many thousands of Gentiles only to let them perish like the beasts ? (Let us mercifully assume that Paul believed in annihilation rather than in future pain). May he not have wondered when the predictions of the prophets would be fulfilled ? And, on the practical side, may he not have perceived how difficult it was for a Greek to become a complete Jew, and how inadequate was the compromise of the ' God fearers ?' May he not have realised that it was almost impossible for the outsider and the outlander to observe the traditions of the fathers, and to practice the enactments of a Law which, taken as a whole, was the Law of a nation and not a Law for mankind ?

And here we enter into the polemical ground which Dieterich, Reitzenstein and other great scholars have opened up for us. The last two questions do not, perhaps, imply ideas too modern for Paul to have conceived, or, in order to make the chasm between Saul and Paul less huge, do not antedate and foreshadow improperly, when we remember that religions, or phases of religion, existed in Paul's day and in his country which deliberately sought to break

down the barriers of race, and to offer one
and the same method and kind of salvation
to all men, whether Greek or barbarian,
whether bond or free. What the false gods
of the heathen in their mysteries offered and
attempted should surely be provided by
the one true religion of the one real God.
But could the Law of Israel be the Law of
all mankind ? And even if this was not
intended, if the Law in its entirety was for
the Jews alone, was this permanent distinction between Jew and Gentile satisfactory ? By what rites, or laws, or methods
were the Gentiles to draw near to the
common God ? I see no certain reason why
this big mind, this versatile and nimble wit,
this sensitive genius, should not have been
harassed by these troubles and questionings,
while yet seeing no clear way out and no
obvious solution, and stifling his doubts in
a still intenser loyalty and devotion to the
Law.

And was there not another point about
the ' mystery religions ' which may have
given him food for strange and painful

I

reflections ? We have seen that Paul could
not have possessed that quiet and balanced
confidence of Rabbinic Judaism in virtue
of which any good man, while lamenting
his frailties and repenting his faults, yet
sought to do his best, and was content to
leave the issue of his fate, in happy trust,
to the judgment of a merciful God. Paul
knew a different and an inferior Judaism,
more anxious and pessimistic, more sombre
and perplexed. He was obsessed by the
sense of human frailty and sinfulness : he
had discovered no remedy strong enough to
cope with the Yetzer ha-Ra, the evil impulse, the wicked promptings of the heart.
God was not near and loving enough for
him as He was to the Rabbinic Jew ; repentance and the Day of Atonement did
not enter so deeply into the very make and
texture of his being ; the good impulse,
(the Yetzer ha-Tob), the righteous promptings of the heart, were less real to him. To
the Rabbinic Jew repentance and forgiveness were forces greater than sin, greater
than the evil inclination, while the ' joy of

the commandments ' was potent enough to
drive away the gloom of occasional and
inevitable failure. To Paul this was not so.
He was no Rabbinic Jew, and of the Law
he knew little more than the fetters, however, great and binding he deemed them :
to him they had not been transformed into
the robe of glory, or transfigured into the
crown of joy. He knew the struggle, but
unlike the Rabbinic Jew, he did not know
the humble triumph, the inward balm :
somehow or other, however ' blameless ' in
the Law's enactments, these had not yielded
to him that sense of rapture and sanctification which no repetition of them, however
frequent, could dim or stale to the Rabbinic
believer. He had always the horrid feeling
of the unconquered evil inclination gnawing
within his soul.

All this is, I admit, pure assumption and
inference, but to account for the Epistles
we are forced to make use of these, and to
bring the imagination into play. If, then,
something like this were accurately to
represent the state of Paul's mind and the

quality of his religion, may he not have cast a wistful eye over the border, where the votaries of the Hellenistic mystery religions were claiming that they could conquer sinfulness at a bound ? Those who with humble faith passed through the rites of initiation were mysteriously re-born ; they died to live again ; they were endowed with a fresh and supernatural strength ; they were invested with a new personality, which enabled them to conquer, and rise superior to, the solicitations of sin. The god had entered into them, and under the appearance of the old body there now dwelt a divine spirit, the source of a new and a higher life.

It is admitted on all hands, though by some reluctantly, that the terminology of Paul shows the influence of the theology of the ' mysteries.' But did he use the terminology without knowing something about the ideas which underlay them ?[1] Doubtless

[1] I have quoted words of Loisy on this point in the Appendix. I might also have quoted from Reitzenstein's already classic article in the Zeitschrift für neutestamentliche Wissenschaft, 1912 (p. 1-28). Reitzenstein shows, on the one hand, that a mere use of phraseology without any influence of the ideas

he thought the whole business false and
blasphemous and unclean, but for all that
he may have felt some secret allurement,
some half-conscious interest, some hidden
feeling, ' how grand it would be if there
were a means of becoming *really and truly*
a new creature, of triumphing over sin and
the Yetzer ha-Ra and the evil heart once
and for all !'   Then one would have received
that new heart and that new spirit which
the Prophets had declared was to be the
gift of God to Israel in the Messianic age.
And that new spirit was to be God's spirit.
The new personality would, in that sense,
be divine.   No longer need one sin, no longer
need one be told in many enactments what
to do and from what to refrain ; the divine
spirit, the new heart, would assuredly
impel towards the right.

The conversion at Damascus must have
befallen a man who was not wholly satisfied
with the inadequate form of Judaism in

which underly them is, under all the circumstances, well nigh
impossible.   On the other hand, it is not a question of
borrowing.   It is a question of the subtlest form of unconscious
influence.

which he had been brought up. He did not know God, as his Rabbinic brethren knew Him, as a loving Father, near, compassionate, forgiving. Then to this mobile, eager, yearning soul, with his gloomy and pessimistic religion, comes the great illumination. Jesus of Nazareth was the Messiah, the Son of God. So much is sure, and soon the key for all difficulties, the solution of all troubles, the attainment of all desires, are found in that one great fact. A new power and hope have come into his life, flooding his whole soul with light and joy. If he feels himself transformed, endowed with a strength and an assurance that he has never known before, why should not this great truth do to others all that it had done to him, and why should he not help to bring it home to them ? Here is the new life, here is the true mystery, through which all alike, whether Jew or Gentile, may attain to the conquest of sin.

Here is the way out. Believe, surrender ; humbly accept. Be convinced that you have no effective power or capacity of your own to crush the sinful desire and to become righteous ; realize that it is only the grace of God and the acceptance, in devout faith, of Jesus Christ as the Messiah who died to free you of your sins, which will clear you in the eyes of God, and will give you the capacity for a new and holy life. Believe in Jesus Christ, and you shall become a new creature ; within you shall now be that new heart and that new spirit, which the prophets foretold, and which alone can make you free. The votaries of the mysteries are trying to get from idols and false gods what can only be got from the One True God, the God of Israel, who is also the God of the spirits of all flesh. In the death and in the resurrection of His divine Son (remember that to Paul, the Hellenistic Jew, the Messiah was a divine being), lies the only efficacious mystery. With him all men must die, in order that with him all may live. Here is the true dying to live. Here are the true I in Thee and Thou in Me.[1]

---

[1] Cp. the section on Paul in Bousset's new book, Kurios Christos, (1913).

So far, so good. So far seems psychologically, on the basis of what has been already said, tolerably clear and satisfactory. And we can understand too that when Paul felt that a new strength, a transfiguration of his whole nature, had come to him from his faith in the risen Christ, he might well have argued : ' By your own efforts, apart from this new power, you cannot fulfil the Law. To try is hopeless. You are doomed to failure. The strength for righteousness can only come to you by the grace of God, and the grace of God and the Spirit of God will only be given to you if you believe in His Son.'

But why did Paul oppose faith in the Son to the works of the Law ? We can now understand him when he says : you cannot do righteous acts, or live a righteous life, without faith in the Son (because you will not receive the necessary power). But if you have the faith, and therefore receive the power, why should you not *then* seek to fulfil the Law ? Why this opposition of faith to works ? Why not say that you can

only accomplish works by means of faith ?
Rabbinic Judaism thought highly of faith,
but never dreamed of opposing it to the Law
or to the works of the Law.

To begin with, Paul, like most other
religious teachers before the modern period,
would have denied that anybody had, or
could have, *any* faith if he had not the *same*
faith as himself. If a Jew had said to him,
' I *have* faith, faith in God who gives me
strength to fulfil his Law, faith in God who
will justify and forgive me if I try my best,
and repent of my faults. But I have no
faith in Jesus of Nazareth, who was not the
Messiah, and whose supposed intervention
between me and God was totally needless,'
Paul would have answered, ' Your faith is
no faith. *Orthopistis* is *my pistis.* There can
be no faith in God which is not also faith
in His Son.' Thus those who clung to the
Law and those who clung to faith in Christ
must inevitably draw further and further
apart, and the way of works would be
opposed to the way of faith.

But far more must the opposition to the

Law and to its works be connected with Paul's conviction that the new religion was intended for *all*, and that God's long-delayed mercy was to bring salvation to every believer in the divine Son, whether Greek or barbarian, whether Gentile or Jew. The barriers of race are to be thrown down: there is to be complete religious equality. But how can there be equality if the Jew is to boast of his Law and of his privileges ? And how can one expect all the world to observe the religious customs of the Jews, customs which, as Paul well knew, if they proved attractive to a Jew, were to many Gentiles a subject of contempt and derision? If all the world *cannot* obey the Law, then all the world *need* not obey the Law.

Would not this point, when reached, have been enough for the mobile and powerful mind of Paul ? The theories could now have an incitement from which to start. And theories in plenty were devised. Some of them have already been noticed. There were also others.

Abraham, even to the Jews, was the

father, the 'patron-saint' of proselytes. How did he win acceptance from God ? Not by the works of the Law, but by faith. Let all the new proselytes do like Abraham, who lived before the Law, and reached his righteousness without it. The law-men reject faith.   Let the faith-men reject the Law. If the believers in Christ attempt to practice the ritual commands of the Law, this means that they think something else necessary to salvation over and above, and beyond, their faith in the Son. But this is to doubt the all-sufficiency of the Son and of his potency for salvation. Therefore to observe the Law is a lack of faith.

But what purpose has the Law ? The old religion is still strong enough in Paul to make him (usually) remain convinced that the Law was holy and good. Its purpose must clearly have been temporary. The patriarchs did, and did well, without it. They had faith. The Law came in between in order to bring about the need for Jesus Christ and his redemptive work. The unbelief of the Jews makes it clear that

the Law does not prevent them being
wicked.   What an illuminating flash it
must have been to Paul when he said, ' Not
prevent them being wicked! Clearly more!
It was *intended* to make them wicked!'
An illuminating flash indeed! As of old
the wickedness of the Amorites had to be
made full, so now the wickedness of the
Jews had to be made full, so that Christ
might appear and redeem all mankind by
his death and resurrection.   Without the
Law there would not be enough sin.   Without enough sin there would not be adequate
occasion for Christ.

As the Gentiles had a certain natural law
of their own, and could sin and did sin, it
would not seem to matter much what took
place in one small tribe in Palestine.   In the
immense sinfulness of the whole Gentile
world, there was, one would have imagined,
enough sin and to spare to secure the coming
of the Christ.   But Paul, while in some
respects ' universal ' in his thought, naturally looks at Jewish history as the centre
of the world.   And we can see how, with ill

success and in a confused way, he yet tries somehow to connect the Law of Moses with the general and increased sinfulness of all humanity.

Every now and then, in his bitter antagonism to the Law and to the Judaizers, he goes even further, and the Law, which he usually regarded as holy and good, came near to being something which is neither good nor holy. For, after all, was the Law *really* given by God as the Jews so frantically assert? Was it not rather given by angels? And are its ritual laws after all so perfect and divine? Did not Jesus say: ' Not that which goeth into the mouth defileth a man?' Of a surety, and in spite of the Law, there is nothing unclean of itself. And does not the Law include enactments which are suspiciously like features of that heathen worship with which we are all familiar? Does it not hallow times and seasons even like the religions of the Gentiles? What are such things but ragged remnants that can now be cast away? Poor elements and beggarly rudiments which the new knowledge and the fuller light can enable us to reject and to discard ! So we may think of Paul advancing from point to point, from argument to argument, and from paradox to paradox, in his conflict with opponents, upon whom he went so far as to utter the imprecation, so amazing on Jewish lips, ' I would that they who trouble you would even destroy their virility !' Could a Rabbinic Jew, even in the violence of his anger, have uttered so remarkable a malediction ?

Thus so far as one can get behind a great genius and an uprooting, illuminating religious experience, one can best explain the Epistles by assuming, first, that Paul's pre-Christian religion was poorer, colder, less satisfying and more pessimistic than Rabbinic Judaism ; secondly, that a special feature of that poorer religion was its more developed and less ' human ' conception of the Messiah ; thirdly, that Paul was already anxious and worried as to the fate of the Gentile world and the great mass of Gentile sinners ; fourthly, that his pessimistic outlook drove him to gloomy views about the power of the 'evil inclination' and the impossibility of overcoming it; fifthly, that his knowledge of the mystery religions made him ready and eager to discover a universal method of salvation, suited and pre-destined for all men, whether Gentile or Jew. His profoundly religious nature had not been given the nurture it required. The near Rabbinic God, who longs to forgive His erring children at the first sign of repentance, was unknown to him. And so perhaps it may conceivably be that the usual interpretation of the 7th chapter of the Epistle to the Romans may not be wholly without validity. Paul may perhaps have yearned to fulfil God's Law, but may have never felt absolutely sure that he had fulfilled it. If guilty in one point, was he not, in God's eyes, guilty in all? He passionately longed to find God, but perhaps he had no profound assurance or conviction that he had found Him. The very things, such as peace and happiness and the presence of God, which to Rabbinic Jews were given by the Law, the Law, to this Hellenistic Jew, seemed perhaps powerless to give. May he not have thought, ' Oh for a way, such as these pagans falsely claim that they have found, a way which would indeed cleanse me of my sinfulness, which would indeed make me right with God, which would indeed enable me to walk in the paths of holiness. The followers of Jesus of Nazareth claim that their Teacher has taught them a higher righteousness than has yet been known. Can it perchance be that these despised sectaries are right ?' And then there came the vision at Damascus, and the way for which he yearned was revealed and made clear to him for ever. Lastly, with the duty imposed upon him by God to preach to all the world the Gospel of the divine Son, he was met by Jewish antagonism and hostility. The new truth becomes not merely the complement of the old religion and its fulfilment, but in one important sense its direct antithesis and contrary. The Law is the strength of sin.

Christianity is not the Law *plus* Jesus Christ. It is Jesus Christ alone : it is the end of the Law and of its bondage it is the advent of the Spirit and of liberty. The letter, which is the Law, kills and leads to death : the Spirit, which is the Lord, gives life and leads Godward. Thus Judaism and Christianity become utterly severed and sundered from each other. The saints of either religion refuse to believe in the possibility of sainthood in the other. In Abraham's bosom each would be surprised to meet the other. But God, who is above and beyond these human limitations, is not surprised at all.

K

THE RELATION OF ST. PAUL TO LIBERAL JUDAISM.

THE way in which the liberal Jew of to-day approaches the study and valuation of Paul is necessarily peculiar. He does not approach the study quite in the same way as a modern Christian would approach Mohammed or Buddha. Neither Buddha nor Mahommed was ever a Christian ; but Paul was born a Jew, remained a Jew for many years, and finally, in a religious sense, ceased to be a Jew, and even became an uncompromising opponent of Judaism. Thus it is obviously easier for a Christian to be an impartial student of Buddha and even Mahommed, than for a Jew to be an impartial student of Paul.

Or let us compare the attitude of a Buddhist who begins the study of Isaiah with the attitude of a Jew who begins the study of Paul. Can they be the same? The Buddhist who studies Isaiah has clearly many advantages over the Jew who attempts a study of Paul. He stands outside and above his subject. He is not concerned, as the Jew would probably be, to gloss over, to apologise, to explain away. Quite simply and easily he can say exactly what he thinks Isaiah meant, and he can state quite frankly whether he agrees with it or not, whether he thinks it good or bad, true or false, valuable or obsolete. He is not concerned to give spiritualized meanings to any unpleasing materialisms. Ragged edges can be left ragged. Rough places need not be smoothed down. Inconsistencies need not be ignored. There will be no need to read a number of modern interpretations into the ancient text. On the other hand, certain relics of still earlier thought which the Jew might not notice and mind—he has been accustomed to them all his life—the Buddhist student will notice at once, and very likely he will ' mind ' them a good deal. He can be placidly critical and uncompromisingly impartial. Yet, if he is not the sort of Buddhist who thinks that his own religious literature has the monopoly of religious excellence and truth, he will be able to notice and emphasize all the good and fine things in Isaiah. He will never want to rob the Jewish prophet of his true worth. He will seek to assess him as he truly was. He will say : ' Here is a fine idea, here is a noble utterance ; this point we Buddhists might well adapt, that conception we might well adopt.' And again he might say, ' Here is a splendid and noble thought, though it lies outside the range of my own religious system ; though I cannot accept the truth of the facts upon which it rests, none the less I admire its beauty, none the less I observe and realize its religious potency and influence.'

Can the modern and liberal Jew study Paul in the same spirit as our imaginary Buddhist has been supposed to study Isaiah ? It may be that the Jew is both too near Paul and too far from him to do him justice or even adequately to understand him. The ashes of old controversies may still glow within the Jew's mind and heart.

Just as it is so very hard for the Christian, even the modern, liberal, quite unorthodox Christian, such as a German professor of theology, to understand and appreciate the Rabbinic religion, so may it also be very hard for the modern, liberal, quite unorthodox Jew to appreciate and understand Paul. It may, therefore, be that this brief essay of mine will have no value or accuracy whatever. Probably all the things which I shall say on the one side will seem false to the Christian and correct to the Jew, while all the things which I shall say upon the other side will seem correct and obvious to the Christian, false and exaggerated to the Jew. Whether such conclusions might indicate that I have hit the mark, or that I am wrong all round, is difficult, and perhaps hopeless, to decide.

The modern and liberal Jew has undoubtedly an enormous amount to reject in the Pauline Epistles. So his impartiality may seem at once to be in fault. Yet these things must be mentioned because they are essential portions of Paul's theology taken as a whole. Moreover they are things *over and above* the one great special point which divides the Christian from the Jew. They have nothing to do with the Messiahship of Jesus, or with his nature, office and work. They are things which the modern and liberal Jew rejects—which are a ' stumbling block ' to him—not so much because he is a Jew as because he is ' liberal ' and ' modern.'

How much of Pauline theology is connected with a conception of the Old Testament that has passed away for ever ! Adam has disappeared ; so have his fall and his sin, and their effects. The resurrection of the body has gone. All ideas of a devil and of powers of evil, or of ' a god of this world ' (the most un-Jewish phrase in Paul), have utterly vanished. Once more, the dualisms of Paul, not so bad as the dualism of the fourth Gospel, but still bad enough, are remote from us. ' Vessels of wrath created for destruction.'[1] How far is even Pauline

---

[1] ' Fitted ' is hardly a strong enough word. ' Prepared ' might do. Lietzmann púts ' geschaffen.'

universalism from ours! We refuse to
admit that those who disagree with us
religiously are 'natural' men, and that we
who have the truth are 'spiritual.' All
men are for us children of God, and all are
created in his image. If this were so—Paul
might argue—the whole need for the incarnation and the death of the divine Son
would disappear. And here we should
entirely agree with Paul, showing in our
agreement the immensity of our diversity.
Still more would the necessity for this
tremendous episode in the history of man
disappear, if we reject, as reject we do, his
doctrine of divine wrath. For the God we
worship had no need to be propitiated by
the blood of Christ. For there was never a
long period of divine anger which had to
be cured by this amazing device. God was
always compassionate. The difficulties of
Theism are as great to us as they were to
Paul. Indeed we realise their difficulties
far more acutely than he. But we, nevertheless, believe in a 'good' God. Only a
good God for us means that all men must

always have been, and always must be, ' saved,' and that the very words wrath and anger are, perhaps, meaningless as applied to God. But if all men are ' saved ' whether they believe in Christ or reject him, whether they are idolaters or monotheists, the basis of Pauline theology collapses. The whole scheme and fabric tumble like a pack of cards to the ground. And so for us modern liberal Jews, they do.

To these general disagreements must be added the specific Jewish disagreement as regards the Christology. Like the Rabbinic Jews of Paul's own day, we disbelieve in this pre-existent divine being, who, though not God, was ' in the form of God,' and emptied himself and was made in the likeness of men. We do not believe that this pre-existent divine being was, during his brief stay on earth, Jesus of Nazareth. We do not believe that he reconciled man to God, because we hold that there was no need of any external reconciliation. So all this central doctrine falls completely away. And though we modern, liberal Jews are not in

Paul's sense, or in the sense of our orthodox co-religionists, ' under the Law,' we nevertheless reject Paul's doctrines of the *work* of Christ in regard to that Law, and of the relation of the Law to sin. Thus, a great deal of what Paul writes has, it must be freely admitted, no value for us : it has not only no value, but it has no present-day interest. It needs some effort on our part to seek to understand Paul, because when we have read him and the best modern commentaries with every care, there is so much which is for us so crude, so remote, so false, so unworthy of God, so valueless for ourselves.

A long discussion concerning the sort of sin which Adam sinned, the sort of sin which people sinned between Adam and Moses, the sort of sin which Jews sinned between Moses and Christ, is wearisome to us. To us the Law is no sudden revelation. Hence the division of the world before and after the Law seems to us mechanical. Paul's confused and often inconsistent reasoning, with its various gaps and omissions, is inclined to bore us. We are so far from his point of view, and to our own mind so enormously beyond it !

Paul's psychology is not ours. His doctrine of sin is not ours. His various ragged edges are clear enough to us, but they do not greatly concern us. What happened to humanity between Adam and Moses ? What happened to all the Gentiles between Moses and Christ ? Did they *all* sin, and were they *all* annihilated at death ? We can recognise that Paul leaves these gigantic questions open, and that his ' theory ' is ragged indeed, but though so much the worse for the theory, we are not otherwise affected. It worries Paul dreadfully that any Christian should sin : theoretically they ought not to sin any more. We do not trouble : we pass on. Paul appears to think that if everything is all right *in the end*, God's kindness as well as His justice are triumphantly vindicated. If all those persons (so he seems to imply) who survive upon the earth when Christ comes again, 'believe' and are saved, the

result appears to him to be highly satisfactory. The heaps of people who must
have gone to perdition, or been annihilated
at death, between Adam and the second
coming of Christ, seem to give him no com-
punction or anxiety. We need not bother
about this curious attitude of mind, except
to remember that we too, like Paul, are
often too apt to gloze over the awful burden
which our Theistic faith is called upon to
bear. We talk of the progress of man, and,
like Paul, are sometimes disposed to think
that if all turn out right in the end, every
difficulty has been overcome. *But what of
all the wreckage on the road?* Does even
the doctrine of immortality account and
compensate for this? Anyhow, we are
far less easily satisfied than Paul, for our
eyes are much wider open than his.

I will omit a number of details—various
superstitions, outworn views about marriage,
celibacy, women, slavery, and other inci-
dental divergencies. Yet in a complete
estimate they would all need to be taken
into account. It is the general point of

view, however, in which the difference
between us and Paul is most glaring and
oppressive. Paul sees no difficulties where
we see many ; on the other hand, he is
pessimistic where we are inclined to be joyful. We believe in the divine goodness so
intensely that the ' evil ' of the world is a
sore burden to our faith, whereas to Paul
the evils are a mark of the ' wrath ' in which
we totally disbelieve. Yet to us, no less
than to the Rabbis, this world (in spite of
evil) is good. God rules it. Creation is
not, and has not been, subjected to vanity.
The earth as well as the heavens declare the
glory of God. Like the Rabbis, we smell
the rose, and thank God for its fragrance.

Is, then, anything left over ? What a
mass we have rejected ! Paul's pessimism,
his Christology, much in his conception of
sin, his conception of the Law, his conception of God's wrath, his demonology, his
view of human past and human future, have
all gone by the board ! What possibly
can remain ?

It may be, however, even in the very

doctrines which we reject, that there are fragments worth preserving. There may be a good deal to adapt, although comparatively little to adopt. There may be matters for appreciation and admiration, though not for complete and absolute agreement. And Paul's doctrine is so rich, he says so many things, that in spite of all that we have rejected, several elements of value may remain over. Lastly, some of Paul's imperfect teachings may point forward to conclusions which we have reached in another way, and along a different road. It remains then to consider and set forth what, in the eyes of a modern and liberal Jew, may counterbalance, (at least to some extent), all that he regards as obsolete or valueless or false. And this is by far the more important and interesting portion of our task. What is positive is so much more pleasant and useful than what is negative. What we can find to care for and use in a great man's writings is so much more absorbing than what we have to reject and cast away.

The heat and bitterness of the old conflict have vanished. We need remember them no more. And so from the very doctrines and sayings which caused or expressed that conflict, we of to-day, heirs of Paul's antagonists though we be, and still rejecting the corner stone of his teaching, can draw profit and suggestion.

So, for instance, the modern and liberal Jew has reached a universalism far broader than Paul's. For we say, ' all are equal before God ' whatever their creed, whereas Paul left those who did not accept the Son in the outer darkness. To us there is no outer darkness, and the mercies of God are for us not limited by race or by creed, by belief or by unbelief. But though we have reached this universalism in our own way and along our own lines, we can recognise the greatness of the advance which was made by Paul, even while regretting that the light of that advance was dimmed by its own painful shadow. The prophetic universalism was made grander and more definite by such sayings as, ' There is no distinction between Jew and Greek ; for the same Lord is Lord of all, and is rich unto all that call upon Him.' ' Is God the God of Jews only ? Is He not the God of Gentiles also ? yea, of Gentiles also : if so be that God is One.' In a sense we do not need these words, for they make no addition to our *present* faith. There is nothing fresh in them to adapt or to adopt. But we cannot read them, I think, without a thrill of admiration. We do not for a moment ignore the traces of universalism and the many universalistic sayings in Rabbinic literature : still less do we ignore the movement and the leanings towards universalism in Hellenistic Judaism. But we perceive that, actually and historically, and in the *fullest* sense theoretically and verbally, universalism was never preached and practised up till Paul's day as it was preached and practised by him. It was attained at a big price : it was attained, moreover, by the forging of a fresh particularism. Still attained it was. And we liberal and modern Jews have to consider

how far our yet wider *theoretic* universalism can or should be matched by a
practical universalism as well. Paul's practical universalism was obtained by the
abolition of Judaism. Can our practical
universalism be won with its retention?

Theoretically we are on perfectly firm
ground. We merely substitute God for
Christ. ' There is no more Jew nor Greek,
there is no more bond nor free : there is
no more male nor female ; but all are one
in '—God. And again, ' where there is
not Greek and Jew, circumcision, and un-
circumcision, barbarian, Scythian, bond-
man, freeman : but ' God ' is all and in all.'
Even to-day such grand and true words
have for us their lesson and significance.
And we can surely recognise not only the
immense influence of the Pauline teaching,
whereby a universal Theistic religion was
definitely established, but also, in spite of
the shadows, the greatness of that teaching
itself. In truth, Judaism could not become
a universal religion together with its in-
violate Law. It remains to be seen, now

I.

that liberal Judaism has adopted an attitude towards that Law very different alike from that either of Paul or his antagonists, whether Judaism can, in practice as well as in theory, be transformed into a universal creed. Such a future for it may be very distant : have we courage and faith enough to work for its coming ?[1]

Let us now pass on to a feature in the Pauline doctrine which seemed to him fundamental, and in sharpest contrariety to the old and superseded religion. According to Paul there is absolute opposition between the method of the Law and the method of Faith. One can seek to put oneself right with God, and to win salvation, by attempting to fulfil the works of the Law; or one can put oneself right with God, and win salvation, by faith. The first method is doomed to failure : the second can be successful. But apart from the inevitable failure of the first, and the practically certain success of the second, this further

---

[1] A learned friend observes : ' The day of " universal creeds " is passing away. Community of conduct, not of thought, will be the link in the future.'

fact is of importance. A combination of
the two methods is impossible. If you have
faith, you are free from the Law ; and if,
pretending to have faith, you coquette with
the Law, you have no true and adequate
faith. Unfortunately, it is impossible to
give a full statement of Paul's doctrine of
faith: this would need an essay to itself.
I have to assume a general and sufficient
acquaintance with that doctrine, and this
assumption is troublesome, because even a
modern and liberal Jew is usually very
ignorant of Paul, and especially ignorant
of what he exactly means by faith. The
liberal, no less than the traditional,
Jew is inclined to think that it means
no more than a mere intellectual acceptance of the facts that Jesus was the
Messiah, and that he ' was delivered up
for men's trespasses, and was raised for
their justification.' He thinks it means an
intellectual acceptance, (1) of certain supposed historical incidents, (2) of certain
alleged theories concerning these incidents;
just as a man might say, ' I fully and sin-

cerely believe that the battle of Hastings was fought in 1066, and that the effect of that battle was to change the character of the English language for ever.' Now it is true that the intellectual element enters into the Pauline doctrine. Paul says : ' So if thou shalt confess with thy mouth that Jesus is the Lord, and shalt believe in thy heart that God raised him from the dead, thou shalt be saved.' But the matter does not end there. Paul means by faith much more than mere intellectual acceptance of certain alleged facts and theories. We mean more than that ourselves when we speak of faith in God. We mean a faith which has an effect upon character. We mean a faith which is a vital portion of our whole being and nature, the dissolution or breakdown of which might, and even would, mean a complete change of outlook, bearing, disposition, and motive. A living and powerful faith in God may supply the whole hidden key to a man's point of view and manner of action. It can stimulate, humble, strengthen, console. It may give the force necessary for noble deeds and steady and sustained purpose. And the change from an incapacity to believe in God to a strong belief in His existence and goodness may exercise the most tremendous effect upon the whole moral and spiritual nature of man. If we learned that, after all, the old views about the battle of Hastings were wrong, and that William was defeated at that battle and not victorious, we should be intensely surprised, but our moral and spiritual nature would hardly undergo any change, whether for better or for worse. Some such wide effects for good, some such broad change in character and outlook, in strength and hope and purpose, were thought by Paul to follow from the ' faith ' in Jesus the Messiah. And doubtless to him such good effects did follow from his new and rapturous conviction.

If, however, we to-day possess a conception of God more inspiring and wider, more consolatory and more stimulating, more intimate and more many-sided, than was Paul's comparatively poor Hellenistic conception of God before his conversion, can his doctrine of faith (which is not merely a doctrine of faith as such, but specifically and essentially a faith in the Messiah-ship and redeeming work of Jesus) be of any service and advantage to us ? Our conception of God, so much richer and fuller, so much more helpful and hopeful, than his old pre-Christian conception of God, makes a faith in any extra subordinate divine being unnecessary, while on the other hand we have not even an intellectual belief in the theories about Jesus and his work with which Paul's doctrine of faith is so inextricably bound up. How, then, can that doctrine be of any service or value to us ?

To us, moreover, ' faith ' is not opposed to ' works ' and our conception of the Law or of Law does not bring us into any difficulties with our conception of faith. We can easily harmonise the two. To Paul, faith in Christ was of necessity opposed to faith in the Law, and indeed he would probably have found the collocation of the two terms impossible to understand. For it

was part of his theory—essential to the
ingathering of the nations and to their
being placed upon a footing of religious
equality with the Jews—that Christ's
coming and Christ's work denoted the
termination of the Law's ineffective and
separating *régime*. ' Christ,' as he says,
' is the end of the Law, for he brings
righteousness to all who believe.' The
holy life, which the Law ordered, but
ordered vainly, Christ can cause to arise
in the soul of all who will believe in him
with full trust and self-surrender. To the
righteousness which the Law ordained, but
did not and could not produce, Christ for
all his followers can show the way. The
Law put men wrong with God, because
through the Law they sinned ; Christ, to
those who believe in him, puts men right
with God, initially and immediately in the
very act of faith, and continuously and
permanently, because now they need sin
no more.

The Pauline theory of faith has for its
necessary correlative the Pauline theory of

the Law. If the one falls, the other, as a whole, falls also. But his theory of the Law was false to the facts of Rabbinic Judaism, and even to some phases of that poorer Hellenistic Judaism amid which he lived. It is obviously, therefore, still more false, or rather still more inapplicable, to ourselves. The theory of faith and the theory of the Law go together, and with them must be associated the conception and theory of grace. Just as Paul opposes ' faith ' and ' Law,' so he opposes ' Law ' and ' grace.' In the new order the believer is no longer under the Law, but under grace. To the man who seeks to do ' works ' under the Law, his reward is reckoned as a ' debt ' due to him, and not as a ' grace.' But in the case of the man who entirely abandons any attempt at obtaining salvation by works, and frankly throws himself in faith upon the mercy of Him who can even ' justify ' the wicked, his faith is reckoned to him as righteousness. In other words God of His grace accepts the faith of the believer as if it were deeds of righteousness.

He pardons and overlooks all his previous sins, so that the man is now right with God, and in addition has (by the gift of the Spirit) the mysterious power conferred upon him to do, through faith, acts of goodness and piety.

Now in all this doctrine Paul does partly hit a certain weakness of Rabbinical Judaism, which must also have been a weakness of the Hellenistic Judaism around him. But this weakness was diminished and rendered comparatively harmless in Rabbinic Judaism by other doctrines and by amiable inconsistencies. In the particular sort of cheap and poor Hellenistic Judaism from which Paul was converted to a belief in Jesus the Messiah, these doctrines and inconsistencies seem to have been wanting. They were not wanting to Philo in Alexandria; they were, as it would appear, wanting to Paul of Tarsus.

The weakness was due to a defect in the quality of any legal religion. There was a certain tendency to take a mechanical view of righteousness and wickedness, as if righteousness consisted in the doing, and as if sin consisted in the omission or the violation, of so and so many separate injunctions. Strike a balance, subtract the good list from the evil, and you can tell, or God can tell, the exact moral condition of any particuliar man. There are undoubtedly several Rabbinical utterances based upon this outward, inadequate, and mechanical conception of righteousness and character, and it is not surprising if the Christian commentators have fastened upon them with much satisfaction. It is unnecessary to point out how such cheap and external valuations of goodness fail to account for the complexity of human character, and how they may directly lead to a lowering of the whole moral and spiritual life.

Character is expressed in, and moulded by, action, but it is something far deeper and more subtle than a number of outward 'doings.' A man may even 'do' little, and 'be' much; he may 'do' much, and 'be' little. A man may have committed no positive sin against the code, and yet he may be a formalist and a hypocrite : at any rate, he may be a poor, empty, negative creature for all his conformity, and for all his scrupulous compliance to the letter of innumerable laws. A man may have committed many faults, and often have lapsed from duty, and yet he may be a noble fellow in the main; he may be one who has done more good, and in truth is worth a vast deal more, than the formal and conventional observer of all the statutes of the code. All this is commonplace and obvious enough to all of us to-day, but it was not so obvious and commonplace to the makers of Rabbinic Judaism.

Then, again, it was rightly felt by these makers of the Rabbinic faith that ' free will ' (in some sense of the words) was at the foundation of morality. Man was free to choose and do either the right or the wrong, and because he was free, he could justly be held accountable, and could become and be called either good or bad. Hence the temptation arose, or, at any rate, it could, logically, have conceivably arisen, to argue that if man ' deserves ' punishment for his voluntary sins, he ' deserves ' reward for his voluntary excellencies. If he has justly ' earned ' punishment for his infractions of the divine commands, he has justly ' earned ' reward for his fulfilment of them. Our own wickedness makes us fail ; our own righteousness makes us succeed. Virtue and vice are within our own power. If we merit punishment, we merit reward. Each will be allotted according to our conformity or disconformity to the code. For every ounce of good and evil we shall receive our deserts.

Whatever measure of truth may lie in this doctrine (and Paul himself does not mind saying that we shall all be judged by our works), the religious mind revolts at it as a whole. It needs to be tempered and combined (at whatever loss of consistency) with other doctrines of a very different kind. By itself and alone it may lead, on the one hand, to pride and false self-sufficiency ; on the other hand, to gloom

and to despair. Paul may have observed
effects of both kinds among the Hellenistic
Jews with whom he was most familiar.
Rabbinic Judaism did, however, possess
ideas and doctrines which, as I have indicated, could, with whatever loss of consistency, temper and prevent the evils of
this moral independence. For it taught,
and believed in, the idea of the divine aid to
human righteousness, and also, though less
pronouncedly, the idea that human virtue
has no ' claim ' upon divine reward. ' For
merit lives from man to man, and not from
man, O Lord, to Thee,' Tennyson's thought
is by no means anti-Rabbinic. If God helps
us to do and to be good, we have no right
to expect a ' reward ' for something which,
in the last resort, is *not* purely ours. And
even as we are not requited (for God is
merciful) according to our sins, so we are
rewarded much beyond our ' merits ' and
'deserts.' Thus ' grace ' enters in on both
sides ; on the one hand, as forgiving and
making allowances ; on the other, as giving
and bestowing far beyond our meed. Rab-

binic Judaism—for its inconsistency is its strength—knew and made use of teachings such as these quite as much as it knew and made use of those doubtful and dangerous teachings of reward and punishment in strict conformity with the accomplished deed. And thus, in actual life, Rabbinic Jews could be and were saved either from despair, upon the one hand, or from pride upon the other. ' God was gracious,' both in forgiveness and in reward. There was comparatively little question of earnings and debts, of merits and deserts.

In the case of the modern and liberal Jew it is obvious that there is less question still. Nobody dreams of boasting to-day of his own ' power,' his own capacities, his own merit, in relation to God. There is no talk or idea of ' debts,' or ' payment ' to be rendered,' and so forth. Faith and grace play a fit and wholesome part in our religious conceptions ; they are neither exaggerated nor ignored. Thus to us, at any rate, Paul seems often to be fighting windmills. He sets up objectionable ninepins that he may knock them down again with his new theories. I believe that even as regards Rabbinic Judaism the ideas he objects to were largely ninepins ; certainly they are so for us at the present day.

Nevertheless it does not follow that Paul's diatribes are of no value even for us. We need both ' law ' and ' grace,' both ' grace ' and ' works,' and though we do not oppose them to one another like Paul, and though we believe that they can form part of a harmonious and co-ordinate whole, it is of value to be occasionally reminded, now of one portion and now of another. Paul, in his trenchant and one-sided way, but with the fervour and eloquence of a great genius and a lofty conviction, reminds us of the one portion, the Rabbinic doctors remind us of the other. We need both ' Being ' and ' Doing.' It is not enough to conform outwardly to a number of moral rules, however excellent. A man needs the inward principle which will make him equal to the varied emergencies that may befall him. The whole soul must be turned to the light, and must itself be luminious. A driving faith is required, or in Paul's words, ' a faith working through love.' Not merely an intellectual acceptance of the principle, but an emotional acceptance of it. The combination floods the whole human nature, and impels it to noble deeds. For if the principle is noble, so will be the deeds that issue from it. Lapses and failures may occur, because the ' faith ' will never be perfect ; the ' flooding ' will never be complete. But the lapses and failures will not be due to ignorance or lack of rules. Given the 'faith' —let us say an acceptance of the doctrine of a righteous and benevolent God combined with a keen love for Him—and there will be little need for rules. The lover of God is learned, even as a human lover is learned. He knows the deeds which are in conformity with his love and with the will of the beloved. Still more, he is not driven to do certain deeds and to refrain from others, because a code, however excellent, says ' Thou shalt ' and ' Thou shalt not,' but he

is driven to do and to refrain, because he
loves, because he has a faith which works
through love.   In complicated situations,
in the actual hurly-burly of life, he has not
to wait and say, ' Under what law do the
present circumstances fall ?'; his principle
his faith, his love, tell him sufficiently how
he is to act.   He is carried beyond the letter
of the law, because love is never satisfied :
whatever he can do can never be enough.
And we may also say that the faith which
works through love is never satisfied.   It
carries a man on to deeds of sacrifice and
supererogation.   It gives the desire to do
these deeds, and the power to accomplish
them.   It prevents the incoming of lower
yearnings ; it overcomes timidity, slug-
gishness and convention.   The flooded soul
is carried forward at a bound, but it
is not only carried forward, but vitally
sustained.   What a mere ' Thou shalt '
or ' Thou shalt not ' cannot achieve, that,
and far more, is accomplished by faith
and love.

Reflections such as these are generated

M

by Paul's doctrine.[1] They may be commonplace, but of some commonplaces it is well
to be reminded. They may also be one-
sided, but it is often necessary to think of
each of the two sides of a truth singly and
separately. We shall not forget the Law
because we also seek to remember Faith.
Having done each of them justice in
artificial isolation, we shall do them better
justice still in combination. On the present
occasion it is unnecessary to enter into a
defence of Law. That must be taken for
granted. ' If man,' as Professor MacCunn
says, ' is not to be the creature of caprice,
he must be made for Law.' The quotation
reminds me to say that for all Jews, whether
orthodox or liberal, the two chapters in
Professor MacCunn's most excellent little
book, *the Making of Character*, entitled,
' Precept ' and ' Causistry ' would supply
most valuable and suggestive reading. They

---

[1] Dr. Abrahams observes : ' We could also arrive at these
reflections from a study of the Hebrew Scriptures and from a
close reading of the Rabbinic Literature. They are in both,
not merely in germ, but in fruit. We need not, therefore,
refuse to be led to consider these points in the presentation
made of them by Paul.'

are entirely untheological, so that no Jewish prejudices could be possibly aroused. The good and the weak points of any moral code are admirable pointed out. And Professor MacCunn shows what, from the liberal Jewish point of view, is extremely sympathetic and agreeable, that it is to Law,—the unwritten moral ideal—rather than to any written code, however excellent, to which our final and ultimate homage must be paid. The supreme court is the Moral Law ; *that* is the Law which makes us free. This is the Law to which we may apply the superb line of Goethe : ' Und das Gesetz nur kann uns Freiheit geben.' Written and formulated precepts, however venerable, however excellent, can only obtain a ' provincial jurisdiction.' There are, then, two Laws, and sometimes, though rarely, as in that moving tale of Franzos, *Nach dem höheren Gesetz*, a man will find that there is an opposition between the one and to other. ' The choice,' as Professor MacCunn puts it, will then be ' between two kinds of law and two kinds of obedience—

obedience to the law of which the last word
is " Thus it is written," and obedience to
that other law which is more enduring and
more imperative than anything that can
ever find adequate embodiment in any
code of precepts.'

What Paul failed to see was that ' faith
which works by love ' could be, and often
was, appended to the very Law which,
with its works, he contrasts with faith. To
the Rabbinic Jew, the Law, as the perfect
gift of the perfect God, was accepted both
intellectually and emotionally. It was both
believed in and loved. And therefore this
faith and this love supplied the very motive
power which Paul had only found when he
became a convert to the new Messiah. He,
with his poorer form of Hellenistic religion,
does not seem to have *loved* the Law ; he
found love elsewhere. But the Rabbinic Jew,
(of 500 A.D. for certain and of 50 A.D. in all
probability), had love already. He could
not break with this love : he could not
disavow this faith. His allegiance was
already given ; a passionate allegiance

which led to noble lives and noble deaths.
He needed no new faith ; the old faith
sufficed.

And we, too, need no new faith. We do
not feel towards the Pentateuch as the Rabbinic Jew felt towards it : but we feel towards God as he felt ; our love for God is
adequate without intercessor. Our faith in
God is adequate without a faith in any
lesser divinity or son. Nevertheless we
recognise the elements of value in Paul's
teaching, and can absorb them. ' Thou
shalt,' ' Thou shalt not ' are still needful
for us : an obligation and a compulsion,
before the majesty of which we bow down
in self-surrender and adoration. But ' the
faith which works through love ' must be
ours as well, the faith and the love which,
in one sense, make all law superfluous and
unnecessary. We stand midway between
the Old Covenant and the New as depicted
by the prophet Jeremiah. The Old Covenant
is outward, and rightly so, for God is without as well as within ; the New Covenant is
inward, and rightly so, for God must be

within as well as without. The prophet separated the old and the new too harshly ; so long as man is man, there must always be both old and new. The moral law is always beyond and greater and above ; but always, if gradually, God is helping us to put His law in our inward parts and to write it—more fully and more powerfully—within our hearts.

We know that Paul, while he held that the Law of Moses was itself spiritual, yet denied that anyone, who clung to it and lived under it and by it, could himself be spiritual. Spirit is by him not merely opposed to flesh, but it is also, so far as man is concerned, opposed to law. Thus Paul can say of the Christian (who alone possesses or can possess the spirit), ' But now, seeing that we have died to that which once held us in bondage (*i.e.*, the Law), we have become freed from the Law, so that we serve in the new spirit and not in the old letter.' To ' serve ' the Law is to Paul *ipso facto* bondage, whereas to the Rabbinic Jew to serve the Law is *ipso facto* liberty. And again Paul says of himself, 'we are the servant of a new covenant, not of the letter, but of the spirit. For the letter kills, but the spirit gives life.' The opposition is always the same : on the one side are Christ, spirit, liberty, life ; on the other side are Law, flesh, bondage and death. When we talk of the spirit of the law, or of intrepreting the Law in its spirit and not in its letter, we are using Pauline words, but not Pauline ideas. To Paul there could be no possibility of interpreting the Law according to its 'spirit.' The Law is spiritual, because given by God, but yet, in relation to man and its observance, it is all letter. You must either follow it as a whole unto death, or be free from it as a whole unto life.

Such a violent opposition is clearly of no use for us to-day. Moreover the Pauline particularism, according to which only the Christian believer can possess the spirit of God, is wholly abhorrent to our modern point of view. Hence the greater part of Paul's doctrine of the spirit is vitiated to

us because of its essential narrowness. Yet,
even so, we can still be stirred by his effective
and eloquent contrasts between the spirit
and the flesh, between, as we might say,
the higher and the lower self. These can
still be read by us with profit and edification. We can also find Paul's teaching
helpful in so far as it reminds us of the
connection between goodness and God,
between human righteousness and divine
righteousness. For, so far as we have
framed such conceptions as those of goodness and righteousness, we have framed
them because we are spiritual, and because
the spirit of God is within us. So far as
we are ' free,' it is because of that spirit.
And this spirit is, on the one hand, intensely
our own, the most essentially human thing
about us, on the other hand, it is essentially
divine, and given to us by the great Not-
ourselves, who is all spirit. That is why we
can pray to God to give us His spirit and not
to ' take His holy spirit from us.' That is
why, whatever our efforts, we must needs
be humble, and why our strength for

righteousness is rather ' given ' than ' our
own.'   Thoughts such as these the Pauline
doctrine of the spirit can evoke, or revive,
in us, and so far as it does so, it is of
value.   And, finally, Paul, in striking
phrases, bids us keep our bodies clean and
alert for the sake of the spirit which is
within them.   ' Do you not know that your
bodies are a sanctuary of the Holy Spirit
which is within you—the Spirit which you
have from God ? . . . .   Therefore
glorify God in your bodies.'   And again,
' Do you not know that you are God's
sanctuary, and that the Spirit of God has
His home within you ?'   In the fine personal
passage which concludes the ninth chapter
of the first Epistle to the Corinthians he
says, ' Every man who strives in the games
practices self-restraint in all directions.
They do this to receive a corruptible wreath:
we do it to receive an incorruptible one.
That, then, is how I run, not blindly : I box
not as one who idly beats the air, but I
buffet my body and bring it into bondage,
so that I may not preach to others, but

myself become rejected.' Surely this is a grand plea for the right discipline of the body. It is not a plea for useless and excessive asceticism, but it is a plea for that exact, and possibly exacting, measure of bodily training and bodily restraint which will make the body the finest servant and instrument of the soul.[1]

The modern and liberal Jew stands far away from, and far above, the old controversy between Paul and the Jews as regards the value and the domination of the ' Mosaic ' Law. It is easy to see, from one important and perfectly valid point of view, that Paul was completely in the wrong. The Law gives no indication of its own transitoriness. Its enactments are to be ' statutes for ever throughout your generations.' And in the fulfilment of these statutes the Rabbinic Jew found sonship and liberty, life and joy. Ingenious as Paul's arguments are, they are ingenious and nothing more. It is as impossible for

---

[1]Dr. Abrahams compares the saying of Hillel who, when he went to his bath, declared that he was performing a religious duty, keeping the tenement clean for the soul that was within.

the Rabbinic Jew of the present day to be moved and influenced by them as it was impossible for the Rabbinic Jew of the first century. To try and prove the transiency and imperfection of the Law *from* the Law is much as if you tried to show from *Modern Painters* that at bottom, and even in the opinion of Ruskin himself, Turner was a feeble artist and a failure in landscape.

But those who stand outside the controversy, and can look at Paul and the Law in an historical and impartial way, may nevertheless find crumbs of value in Paul's elaborate periods and denunciations. I have touched already upon the opposition of 'Law' to 'Grace' and to 'Faith.' One more point remains over. It is one which must have very specially aroused the enmity and anger of the Jews. Paul clearly came to believe that the Law was intended for the childhood of the world, and that it was no longer necessary or fitted for the age of spiritual manhood and religious emancipation. The Christian believer, whether Gentile or Jew, is an adult son, free, and conscious of his freedom and of his sonship. Before Christ came, the human world was in tutelage. Men were minors, ' under guardians and stewards until the appointed time of the father.' This tutelage and minority held good both of Gentiles and of Jews : as Paul ascribed to both of them now—when they accept Christ—a complete religious equality, so, in one of his moods at any rate, he is disposed also to assimilate their religious condition before Christ came with his message of sonship and of liberty. The spirit alone gives freedom, and before the days of the spirit, in other words, before the advent of the divine Messiah, all men alike were in bondage and in ward. The religion of the Jews before Christ, the Jewish religion without Christ, sank, therefore, in this mood of Paul's and according to this theory, almost to a level with heathen worships and heathen creeds.

All men alike were sinful ; all men alike were children, differing, as children, little, if at all, from the condition of the servant and the slave. Paul was doubtless aware

of the criticisms levelled by various out-
siders upon the Jewish Law. And as, from
his position of hostility and aloofness, he
looked back upon it, it began to appear
to him as if some of these criticisms were
justified. Some portions of the Law were
like the various cults and worships of the
heathen nations themselves. There was
doubtless divine intention in this, for Jews,
no less than Gentiles, were to be children
and slaves till the universal Redeemer
should be born. But the fact remained.
The ritual of the Law was intended for such
children, and on a par with their religious
and spiritual capacities. So, too, was the
ritual of the heathen. Jews and Gentiles
alike offered sacrifices, observed times and
seasons, made distinctions of food. Though
we cannot prove it, it seems probable that
Paul, with his keen and nimble wit, was
able to realise the similarities, as well as
the differences, between the Jewish ceremonial law and the ceremonial usages of the
heathen. In the three points mentioned,
sacrifices, observances of time and seasons,

and regulations about food, such similarities undoubtedly existed. All three sorts of ceremonial seemed to the eager and passionate mind of Paul, in the flush of his new enthusiasm, alike antiquated and unnecessary. With the faith in Christ, with the regeneration which that faith could and did bring about, and in the possession of the Spirit, what need of such practices, observances, and abstentions ? All such rules and regulations could now be swept away : they were suited to children, but not to adults. Spiritual beings had no need of them. The spirit would bring forth its own fruits without such petty regulations. A spiritual service was the only religion now required and now suitable. Material sacrifices could be abolished for ever ; Christ had made, and he was, the supreme and final sacrifice. Humanity was emancipated and free. And so Paul could say, ' We, when we were children, were held in bondage under the rudiments of the world, but when the fullness of the time came, God sent forth His Son, born of a woman, placed

under the Law, in order that he might redeem those who were enslaved under the
Law, that we might receive the adoption
of sons.' Now that this adoption has been
received, now that the child-slaves, whether
Jew or Gentile, have become sons, there
must be no looking or turning back. The
' rudiments ' belong to a past age ; there
must be no coquetting with them again ;
no vain regrets for the bondage overthrown.
The Gentiles who have come to know God
must not turn back again to the ' weak and
beggerly rudiments,' or desire once more to
be in bondage. They must not observe (as
some had a retrograde desire and tendency
to do), ' days and months and seasons and
years.' This he says in the Galatians, and
if the Colossians are genuine, as is now
generally believed, the same thought is
taken up again here. ' If ye died with Christ
from the rudiments of the world, why, as
though living in the world, do ye subject
yourselves to ordinances, " Handle not,
taste not, touch not," after the precepts and
doctrines of men ?' ' Let no man judge you

in meat or in drink, or in respect of a feast day or a new moon or a sabbath day. They are but a shadow of what was to come. The reality is in Christ.'

Paul's doctrine of the 'stoicheia'—elements or rudiments as the word is usually translated—is full of difficulties, and has provoked pages of commentary and discussion. But however strange it may be to conceive the quondam Jew speaking of a command in the decalogue as a precept and ordinance of men (for this is what his argument, pushed home, would amount to), it seems fairly certain that he does here assimilate Jewish ceremonial ordinances to the similar ordinances of the heathen.

What are we to say from *our* point of view about these arguments and statements ? We shall, first of all, remember that for human beings institutional religion and outward forms are a necessity. And in spite of Paul we shall continue, quite unconcernedly and with deliberate purpose, to observe months and seasons, feast days and sabbaths. Nor shall we fail to perceive in such an institution as the Sabbath, whatever its origin, something more than the precept and doctrine of man. However the Sabbath arose, and whatever its history, the finger of God is in it. Again we shall not be slow to recognise that the dietary laws, though we may not choose to observe them ourselves, have been, and still may be, of distinct value for the discipline of the body and of the will. Paul is wrong if he denies that they can have such uses and effects. But, nevertheless, the Apostle does seem gifted with a certain prophetic vision when he includes some portions of the ceremonial law within the range and compass of 'stoicheia.' For we have now learnt to realise—comparative religion has made it clear—that the Pentateuchal Law includes many a heathen ' rudiment.' Food taboos, laws of uncleanness, circumcision, sacrifices of flesh and blood—these things, and others like them, are not parts of the prophetic religion of Amos and Isaiah, they are not peculiar to Israel, but they belong to an earlier and wider stage of religious develop-

N

ment, and were taken over and incorporated into that compromise of Prophet and Priest which we know as the Pentateuchal or 'Mosaic' Law. Some of them, such as the Day of Atonement, have been spiritualised out of all recognition with their origin in the Law. Some of them, such as the Sabbath and the Passover, were ' historicised ' and spiritualised within the Law itself. But because we can now trace and recognise their non-Israelite origin, because we, like Paul, though on a far wider basis of knowledge and with much greater calm and impartiality, can recognise them as *stoicheia*, we can use them, develop them, amend them, or drop them, to the best religious and spiritual advantage. We too are free in regard to them, though, in and with our freedom, we may choose freely to observe them. A few of us may like freely to practice some of them—such as the dietary laws—which others may think it better to ignore. But, in all cases, we shall act towards them as freemen. Even the Sabbath we shall observe, not according to a series

of rules, but in the ' liberty of the spirit.'
It is possible that, here and there, such an
observance in the spirit may mean in our
day a stricter observance than if we followed
the letter of the Rabbinical Law. Just because we are ' liberals,' we shall not, like
Paul, condemn the Law in essence or as
such. For we regard Law as a revelation of
the divine Spirit continuously at work,
and this very conception allows and justifies our freedom towards the details of the
written code.

Meanwhile, recognising that many ceremonial laws are *stoicheia*, our new attitude
towards them receives its historical and
scientific sanction. In one sense, indeed, it
may be said that all religious ceremonies
and institutions are *stoicheia*. All are
the human embodiments or handmaidens
of spiritual and moral truths. And thus our
relation to all Jewish ceremonial is conditioned by its actual or possible relation to
those moral and spiritual truths. We
recognise the human need for forms and institutions. We recognise that, for a variety

of reasons, we had better use and adapt those which are hallowed by age and by history than create a series of cold and brand-new forms for ourselves. We, therefore, deliberately take over or modify those which best suit our purpose and most fully answer to our needs. And one of those needs is to preserve the historic continuity of our religion and an adequate and outward connection with all our brethren in faith. Such, then, is the use and the development which we make of Paul's doctrine of the rudiments —a very different use from his, a very different and far juster appreciation, but yet one which can find in Paul's doctrine a certain prediction or adumbration of our own.

Paul's theory of the Law is in many ways a perversion of the facts. Nevertheless, we cannot but recognise that for the world at large the Law could only have been a bondage. We perceive now, from a wholly different point of view, that there was a real historic truth in comparing its ceremonial enactments with the weak rudiments of the lower religions. Knowing as we do that there is no written document into which the human mind, as well as the human hand, does not largely enter, we realise that the religious supremacy of such a document, from which there was no appeal, would be unsuited for the matured conscience of humanity. We interpret the Law; we distinguish between what is moral and what is ritual. By the infraction of a single command which it is within his power to obey, every Jew, however disinclined he may be to acknowledge it, has tacitly put himself above the Law, and claimed for his conscience and for his reason the right of interpretation and disobedience. He has put the spirit above the letter, and entered into the world of freedom. ' Where the Spirit of the Lord is, there is liberty.' And this spiritual emancipation is largely due to Paul. The doctrine of that remarkable passage in the 1st Epistle to the Corinthians (ii. 10-16) contains a great truth, however useful it may be to disentangle its per-manent value from its temporary form, and to qualify it with saving provisos. ' He that is spiritual judges all things.' In one deep sense there can be nothing between the human soul and God. Each of us must fashion his own religion.

Though Paul, in his more violent and intransigent moods, appears to admit of no compromise as regards the Law and its works, yet on other occasions, both in theory and practice, he was seemingly willing to do so. During his own apostleship he became, as he himself phrases it, ' all things to all men, that he might by all means save some.' All this he did for the Gospel's sake. Thus to the Jews he ' became as a Jew that he might win the Jews ; to those that were under the Law he became as under the Law that he might gain those that were under the Law.' What Paul means by this statement is not perfectly clear ; but, at any rate, in his intercourse with Jews he must have made certain concessions so as not to offend their ' prejudices,' and in such things as food, and perhaps in washing the hands before partaking of food, he must have conformed to Jewish practice, obeying the Law, not because of the Law or as recognising its rule, but in order that such details might not possibly interfere with the success of his main message. He justifies his action by the admirable counsel and by the wise rulings which he lays down for others both in the Epistle to the Romans and in the 1st Epistle to the Corinthians. The great point is, he says, not to give needless offence. ' Give no occasion of stumbling either to Jews or to Greeks or to the Church of God ; even as I also please all men in all things, not seeking mine own profit, but the profit of the many that they may be saved.'

This principle is elaborately exemplified in the matter of food. He is convinced that 'nothing is unclean of itself.' He, like Jesus, (though it is doubtful whether he depends upon the teaching of the Master), has emancipated himself from all taboos. ' The earth is the Lord's and the fulness thereof.' God has created both the mouse and the cow ; in one deep sense, therefore, the mouse is,

and can be, no less clean than the cow.
Rabbinic Judaism, in spite of the rigidity
with which it clung to the food taboos and
even painfully extended them, had, never
theless, reached this knowledge in its own
way, though on different lines. For, to the
Rabbinic teachers, the mouse was an unclean animal, not in itself, but because God
had chosen to declare it to be so *for the Jews*.
And he had chosen to declare it to be so in
order that by this means, as by all the other
ceremonial means, he might enable the Jews
to purify and discipline their wills. The
laws about food were so many arbitrary
ukases given by supreme wisdom for man's
training and sanctification.

This theory, though for historical and
philosophical reasons it is (at any rate in
its plain Rabbinic form) impossible of
acceptance for us to-day, was an immense
improvement over any view which regarded
the uncleanness of the mouse or of the hare
as inherent in the animal itself.[1] Neverthe-

[1] I leave out of account here what we may call the scientific
side of the question. Some of the old taboos may, for reasons
of health, be still approved by modern science. But the position

less it still left a not wholly satisfactory situation. ' Uncleanness ' (which has by the way nothing to do with unwholesomeness) was, it is true, not due to spirits and demons or to anything dangerous, uncanny and mysterious. But it was nevertheless not wholly imaginary. It was a real thing, arbitrarily created for moral purposes, and from the best and kindest of motives, by God himself. Such is the Rabbinic doctrine. Paul's doctrine goes further. The Christian believer no longer requires such methods of purification. His faith is enough. He must be grown up enough not to need to lean upon such outward crutches. ' Food will not bring us nearer God ; if we eat not, we are not the worse ; if we eat, we are not the better.' ' The kingdom of God is not eating and drinking, but righteousness and peace and joy in the Holy Spirit.'

In the long run the attitude of liberal Judaism towards the dietary laws will, I think, have to be along these lines. We

of modern science towards food in its relation to health is no less far removed from the Pauline, than it is from the Rabbinic, point of view, and perhaps even farther.

shall not for a moment deny that for a Jew who resides in England or America or France, and who lives the ordinary life of an English, American or French citizen, associating freely with his non-Jewish fellow-citizens, travelling, dining out, and so on, the faithful observance of the Biblical, to say nothing of the Rabbinical, dietary laws may be an excellent exercise in self-control. (For the Jew who lives almost exclusively among Jews the self-control involved is extremely small). Nevertheless, the theoretic foundation being removed, it will, I think, be necessary for liberal Jews to train their children in other methods of discipline and restraint. Such methods there are in plenty, and there is little reason to believe that those who observe no dietary taboos need be less self-controlled and less holy in mind or pure in body than those who obey them.

So far, then, we shall be with Paul in his main principle : ' nothing is unclean of itself.' (Many things may be unwholesome in themselves.) We have passed beyond the stage—and we must see to it that our children do not suffer—in which abstention from certain meats can be clearly and satisfactorily associated with religion. For good or for evil (and we must see to it that it shall not be for evil), the kingdom of God is no longer associated with this or that particular animal, or with this or that particular method of slaughter ; however much we may also agree with that other saying of Paul (quite Jewish and Rabbinic), 'whether, therefore, ye eat and drink, or whatsoever ye do, do all to the glory of God.' We shall eat temperately, and for the best discipline and strengthening of the body : we shall eat such foods as the doctor may recommend to us, and as may best happen to suit our particular constitution and the climate in which we live. Such, then, will be *our* dietary laws,' and in their fulfilment we shall best sanctify the natural, spiritualise the material, and 'do all to the glory of God.'

But no less acceptable, and to many of us, doubtless, far more acceptable, than the broad principles of Paul as to clean and unclean, are his cautions and compromises. First of all, no boasting. Even if (paraphrasing Paul) when we eat hare, we are not the worse, yet assuredly we are not the better. Indeed, if we think we can, or must, (lacking their foundation in faith) do without the dietary laws, we have earnestly to see to it that we are not the worse for our 'liberty.' Likely enough our 'unemancipated' brother, if we are not careful, may be the better, And again, so many other things are much more important than dietary laws. There is no need to attack them. If the Liberal Jew chooses to observe the dietary laws—whether Biblical or Rabbinic—let him do so. If they still help him to a holy life and to a more vivid faith in God, let him observe them. 'Overthrow not, for food's sake, the work of God.' And the admirable teaching in the fourteenth chapter of Romans and in the eight and tenth chapters of the first Corinthians gives us excellent practical rules in our general intercourse with our brethren in faith. An outward detail may cause to some people

more difficulty and offence than a theo-
retical truth. To our *principles* we must be
true, and if we are speakers or writers, we
must give expression to them. But it is not
necessary to put them into practice on every
possible occasion in season and out of season.
Some people may readily understand and
appreciate a principle, but not yet be able
to realise its every application. If I am seen
to smoke on a Saturday, I may not only
offend my traditional and orthodox brother,
but I may hurt the conscience of my brother
to whom traditional and orthodox Judaism
has become unreal and impossible of acceptance, but who cannot as yet carry out,
without injury, the principles of Liberal
Judaism in all their applications. He may
not be able to smoke without an injury to
his conscience. I must, then, be careful not
to injure it. He lives to God without smok-
ing on Saturday, quite as much as, and
perhaps better than, I who smoke. So in
the same way, if you eat with him at a
restaurant, you may be able to eat a shrimp
without any injury to your conscience and

in the most perfect freedom : he may not
Will you tempt him to follow your example,
seeing that he cannot yet do so without
sin ? Surely not. ' Let each man be fully
assured in his own mind.' If you eat the
shrimp, you can only eat it without sin, if
you can ' eat it unto God.' ' He that eats,
eats unto the Lord, for he gives God thanks;
he that eats not, unto the Lord he eats not,
and gives God thanks.' Though the shrimp
is in itself clean, and may be clean to you,
it is truly unclean for that man who eats it
with a bad conscience. At such a time,
' the faith which you have, have it to yourself before God.' And even if we feel a little
restraint in acting thus, it may be yet good
and wise. For we, who call ourselves in
such things ' strong,' should rightly bear,
in small outward details, the infirmities of
the weak : we ought not ' to please ourselves.' Our vaunted enlightenment may
so easily puff us up : let us prevent such
conceit (which may have such evil consequences) by the warmth of our love, ' for
love edifies.'

We may equally apply the sensible advice which Paul gives about dinner parties and about meat which has formed part of a sacrifice to a heathen god.   In fact we may extend that advice both to those who follow, and to those who do not follow, the dietary laws of the Pentateuch.   ' If one of them that believe not, ask you to a banquet and you are disposed to go, whatsoever is set before you, eat, asking no question,' Thus if a dish comes before you, which is apparently beef or mutton, eat and ask no questions ; but if the bill of fare or your host informs you that it is made of lobster or hare, then refrain.   If you are an observer of the dietary laws, the reason is obvious ; if you are not, you may nevertheless do well to refrain, either because of a weaker brother who may be present (this is Paul's reason), or because your host may think that, as a Jew, you *ought* to refrain, and your ' liberty,' put into practice, may be to the dishonour, and not to the glory, of God.

The common-sense of the Apostle is shown in another point which, though it has no connection with food, may perhaps also be mentioned here. We may find it of value as a justification for our use of the vernacular in public worship. Paul is writing about the peculiar phenomenon of the first days of the Church, ' speaking in tongues.' He himself ' spoke with tongues ' more than ' any of them all,' but for purposes of true edification he perceives that such speaking is spiritually fruitlesss. Unless you understand what is said, what can be the profit ? ' If I know not the meaning of the language, the speaker is unintelligible to me.' But in prayer there must be understanding. ' How shall the unlearned say Amen to your thanksgiving, if he does not understand what you say ? ' We have to recognise facts as they are ; we have to realise that the main purpose of public prayer is that the worshipper shall understand it. Public prayer is not for the learned few : it is for the average and unlearned many.[1]

---

[1] Dr. Abrahams observes : ' The Rabbis taught the same. Pray in any language was the sum of their teaching. In this respect the later orthodoxy became far more rigid than were the older Rabbis.'

Passing away at this point from Paul's teaching about the Law, let us ask whether, and how far, we are able to find help in, or draw inspiration from, those portions of Paul's doctrine which deal with the reproduction of the death and the risen life of the Messiah in the experience of each individual believer. It may be that we are touching here upon a matter which is too closely and inseparably bound up with a belief in certain alleged events and with their interpretation to be of any value to those who either disbelieve in the events themselves, or interpret them in a very different way. It may be that these elements of Paul's teaching do not bear transplantation to any alien soil or admit of application to any other religion than his own. I, moreover, have a special difficulty in dealing with this portion of my subject, which is peculiar to myself. Convinced as I am that there is great religious value, beauty and truth in mysticism, I, like many, though by no means all, modern Jews, stand outside the mystic limit. There are some who (rashly and foolishly as I

o

think) would deny that there *is* anything
beyond that limit, others who would deny
that what is beyond is more than idle dream-
ing, emotional vagueness, unreal phantasies.
For myself I am convinced that the mystics
of all creeds and races are much more than,
and very different from, irrational and useless dreamers. Nevertheless, the power fully
to comprehend and to appropriate the
thoughts and the language of mysticism
has been denied me. But the portion of
Paul's doctrine which has to do with the
appropriation and imitation of the death
and resurrection of Christ by the individual
believer leads us up into the very heart and
core of the Pauline mysticism. Even a
double outsider like myself—that is, a Jew
who is not a mystic—can to some extent
appreciate its solemnity, its power and its
beauty, but he will hardly be able to appreciate and understand it fully, and still less
will he be able fully to measure or realise
how far it may be capable of adaptation
outside the borders of Christianity.

Paul's doctrine was a combination of

ethical and sacramental teaching. It was allied to the doctrine of the mystery religions, but it was much more thoroughly moralized. The believer who, in full and humble faith, accepted the facts, and the interpretation of the facts, which Paul presented to him concerning the life and death of Christ, would be transformed into a new creature. This transformation was *real*; it was something given to him, brought to him, put into him. If we ask what meaning is to be assigned to the word ' real,' it is not easy to define it. The ' spirit ' which was ' given ' to the believer was not purely ' spiritual ' in our sense of the word. Paul's views about ' matter ' and ' spirit,' about ' body ' and ' soul,' were not quite the same as ours. So, too, he could conceive no satisfactory life after death without a ' body,' upon which, apparently, individuality for him depended. Even a ' naked ' spirit was probably not for him anything so purely immaterial as it would be for us. Something, then, which was real and external to the believer hap-

pened to him when he ' believed,' and when,
as the pledge of his belief, he was baptized.
It may be—the point is disputed—that the
gift of the spirit was even conditional upon
the rite of baptism being undergone. In any
case, God *gave* something to the believer,
though the believer had also to bring something to God. The new life could not be
won without the joint action both of God
and man : and both their actions were
dependent upon the death and resurrection
of Christ having actually taken place.
Christ by his voluntary death destroyed
the domination of sin. What man, and,
it would not seem false to Paul to say,
what God, could not do before, now,
through the death of the Sinless Son,
became possible. God could forgive, and
man could rise. So much we have already
heard, but here is the point which specially
concerns us now. Consistently or not
consistently, Paul usually holds and teaches
that effort is still required. Until the full
transformation after death takes place,
there has to be a combination of effort and

faith. Full faith should really make an injunction such as, ' let not sin reign in your mortal body,' unnecessary. There should be no longer the desire to sin. But Paul never teaches placidity or quietism. He preaches effort, striving, endeavour. And it is precisely the combination of effort and faith which is to produce that moral enthusiasm, that spiritual glow, that mystic conviction, which break out so often in his teaching, and which he sought so earnestly to beget in his disciples.

The new faith was to produce a new man, a new creature. And the new creature was to be, in the first place, a more powerful and a more joyful, as well as a more righteous and more holy, creature than the old. He was to endure sorrow more easily, and to rejoice in tribulation : he was to love more zealously : to live for others more completely. If he *sought* to be all this, he *could* be all this. The power was within him. But even all this is not all. For the mystic element, that animates the whole, has still to be mentioned. The new man is a man who lives unto Christ and unto God, and not only so, but he is united with Christ, and has become one with him. The spirit of God which raised up Jesus from the dead dwells in him, and nothing can separate him from the divine love. Christ is ' in ' him ; the old ' I ' has vanished ; it is Christ, the Son of God, who lives within him now.

It cannot be valueless to read the passages in the Epistles which are penetrated with this white heat of conviction and enthusiasm. Regarded merely as literature, they are magnificent : moreover, such fervent and rapturous words are, to some extent, infectious, even though they may depend upon conceptions which are alien to those that read them. Can we go a little further, and more specifically make use of them ? It is clear that we, like any modern Christian, are born into our faith. There cannot be for us a tremendous severance between old and new. Nevertheless, we can learn to live unto God and not to ourselves ; working for His cause, which is the cause of righteousness, and not merely for our own advancement. We can learn to feel love towards God, and to believe that God loves us : and in the conviction and energy of that dual love, might some of us not be capable of rising to new heights of devotion, sacrifice and enthusiasm ? The ' once born ' and the ' twice born,' the non-mystic and the mystic, can both go thus far together with equal conviction and equal passion. The mystic may pass forward another step, and realise, without the necessity of any half-way house between himself and the Father, that he is in God and that God—or shall we say God's spirit ?—is in him. I do not see why the love of God should not at last so fulfil and constrain a man as to make him humbly declare that, when he compares himself with what he was in older days, before he realised what this love of his towards Divine perfection, and what this love of Divine perfection towards him implied, he must almost regard himself as a new creature, with a fresh and different outlook upon life and eternity. The Rabbis spoke of a

proselyte, brought to the knowledge of the
One God, as new made and re-created. By
a Jew, then, as well as by Paul, it might be
said, 'the old things are passed away;
behold they are become new,' And he
might be grateful to Paul, even though his
own language and conceptions will be so
different from the language and conceptions
of the Apostle. For from every lover of
God, filled also with a fiery zeal for
righteousness, when such love and zeal are
combined with force and genius such as
Paul's, it is surely possible to learn. Admiration is helpful, and, in a certain sense,
it may be contagious. Mysticism is not the
prerogative of one religion only. Given man
and given God, there may be mystics in
every Theistic creed.

Whether, however, we are sympathetic
to mysticism or not, or whether, even though
sympathetic, we are capable or no of understanding it, and of ourselves advancing
some steps along 'the mystic way,' we can
in all cases alike, appreciate, and be stimulated by, those wonderful passages in the

Epistles in which the Apostle speaks of his own feelings and experiences. We cannot but be struck by his remarkable combination of humility and confidence, by his fortitude and enthusiasm, his indomitable perseverance, his high spirits (to use a homely and yet truthful expression), undaunted by difficulties, troubles and pain. There is always something inspiring in the picture of a great man, convinced of his cause, and pursuing his straight course in the face of constant opposition and trial. Paul not only rises superior to his sufferings, but he exults and rejoices in them. And perhaps in this exultation and rejoicing lies the most peculiar and instructive feature of his career, the feature, moreover, in which he was, though perhaps unconsciously, in fullest accordance with the teaching of his Master and his Lord.

These grand autobiographical passages occur in greatest abundance in the two Epistles to the Corinthians, and more especially in the second. So, for instance, in the stirring description of his apostleship : ' We give no cause of offence to any-body in anything, so that our office may not be condemned ; but in all things as God's servants, we commend ourselves,—in much patience, in affliction, in trials, in distresses, in stripes, in imprisonments, in tumults, in labours, in watchings, in fastings ; in purity, in knowledge, in longsuffering, in kindness; in the Holy Spirit, in love unfeigned, in the word of truth, in the power of God ; by the weapons of righteousness on the right hand and on the left, in glory and in ignominy, in good report and evil report ; as deceiving and as true, as unknown and as well known; as dying, and behold we live ; as chastened, and yet not killed ; as sorrowful, yet always rejoicing ; as beggars, yet making many rich ; as having nothing, and yet posses-ing all.'

In a small man this self-commendation and this list of virtues would be offensive and ridiculous ; in a big man like Paul, it is justified, because it is not only true, but spoken at the right time and in the right way. Just because the glory of it is not his, but God's—for so he would regard it—is the pride of it justified, and not incompatible with humility. And the courage the enthusiasm, and the indomitable joy, can be helpful to quite ordinary people to-day. To be stirred by such a passage and by others like them must be of advantage to us. To be ignorant of them, through prejudice, must be a loss. Where else can Jewish readers find such noble bits of auto-biographical literature? Why should they lose the benefit of them? We need not now be deterred from admiring them and *catching the new note in them*,—for surely a new note there is—merely because their author was a born Jew, and wandered far away from the doctrines of Judaism.

I fully admit that in one point Paul often fell below the description which he gives, not in all probability of his sufferings, but of his attitude towards his opponents. In the Epistles, at any rate, there is very little to be found of kindness and blessing towards those who differed from and opposed him. He knew what he ought to have done, but his lower self in this one respect constantly got the better of him. This we cannot quite forget even when we read a noble passage like the following : ' It seems to me that God has exhibited us apostles last of all, as men condemned to death ; for we have become a spectacle to all creation—alike to angels and to men. We are fools for Christ's sake, but you are wise in Christ; we are weak, but you are strong,; you have glory, but we have dishonour. For even unto this very hour we hunger and thirst, and are naked and beaten, and have no certain dwelling-place. We labour, working with our own hands ; being reviled, we bless ; being persecuted, we endure ; being defamed, we entreat. We have become as the scapegoats of the world, the refuse of all things, even until now.' Again, in another place, he says, ' We have this treasure (*i.e.*, the Gospel) in vessels of clay (*i.e.*, his own personality) that men may realise that the surpassing greatness of the power is from God, and not from us. We are pressed on every side, yet not straitened utterly, per-

plexed, yet not unto despair, persecuted, yet
not forsaken, borne down, but not destroyed. . . And so we faint not, but though
our outward man is decaying, our inward
man is renewed day by day. For our light
affliction of the present works for us more
and more exceedingly an eternal weight of
glory ; while we look, not at the things
that are seen, but at the things which are
not seen ; for the things which are seen are
temporary, but the things which are not
seen are eternal.' We, too, with a kindred,
though different, faith, can feel the grandeur
of this last contrast ; we, too, often perplexed, may seek, like Paul, that our per-
plexity may not be unto despair.

Those who labour for any worthy cause
may find suggestion and help in the stead-
fastness of the great Apostle.   Often where
Paul says Christ, we can say God, and to
us the word will seem grander and more
holy. In mental dejection, and in physical
weakness, we can take example from Paul,
when, referring to some distressing infirmity
from which he suffered, he says : ' Concern-

ing this thing I besought the Lord thrice
that it might depart from me. And he said
unto me, My grace must be sufficient for
thee ; for the power perfects itself in weakness. Most gladly, therefore, will I rather
boast of my weakness, that the power of
Christ may rest upon me. Wherefore I
take pleasure in weaknesses, in insults, in
trials, in persecutions, in distresses, for
Christ's sake ; for when I am weak, then I
am strong.' This, not mere fidelity, but
glad exultation in sufferings, meets us
frequently. So in the Epistle to the Colossians, where Paul says : ' I rejoice in my
sufferings for your sake.' It is a privilege,
not merely to believe in Christ, but also to
suffer for him. Under all circumstances,
' rejoice in the Lord always ; again I will
say, rejoice.' It is natural that to any brave
man, with an intense conviction of a future
life, death is robbed of its terrors. Paul
tells the Philippians that for himself he
would prefer ' to depart and be with Christ,
for it is very far better.' But for the sake of
his work, it is more needful that he should

still continue to ' abide in the flesh.' On
the other hand, if his life is to be poured out
as a libation upon the sacrificial offering of
the faith of the Philippian community, he
will ' rejoice.' Whatever befalls him, he is
content. ' I know how to be abased, and
how also to abound ; in everything and in
all things I have learned the secret both to
be filled and to be hungry, both to abound
and be in want. I can do all things through
him that strengthens me.' Truly a noble
and stimulating self-sufficiency. Truly
also a high-hearted and inspiring enthusiasm, an indomitable and inexhaustible
courage. A man who can feel in such a way
had the right to utter the bidding : ' Rejoice always ; in everything give thanks.'
Or again, ' Let no one be moved by these
afflictions, for yourselves know that here-
unto we are appointed.'

The Jewish reader of the Epistles should
surely be able to approach this side of the
Epistles with greater facility and sympathy.
His own teachers have said many fine things
on the same topics. But we cannot, without

serious loss, refuse to regard the good things said by Paul because similar good things (scattered over a huge, unwieldy and not easily available literature) were said by others. Because he finds inspiration in the Rabbis, he should not turn a deaf ear to Paul. For the Jewish student or reader of the Epistles can consider their more purely ethical portions with an un-prejudiced mind. From them he can more easily appropriate all that is good and true. He may, indeed, raise the old, stale quarrel as to priority and originality, but he will hardly deny that such injunctions as, ' Let love be without hypocrisy,' ' Render to no man evil for evil.' 'Be not overcome by evil, but overcome evil with good,' are in them-selves useful and excellent even unto this day. It is not, therefore, necessary for me to dwell upon Paul's ethics at any length. I doubt whether they go much beyond the limit of Rabbinical teaching at its highest and best. But they have these distinct advantages, first, that they are easily available, next, that they are contained within a very small compass, and lastly, that they are nobly expressed, and redolent of enthusiasm and genius. The Jewish critic may laboriously seek to prove that the famous thirteenth chapter of the 1st Epistle to the Corinthians can be paralleled by phrases and thoughts in the Rabbinical literature (at least he will seek to do this when he does not take the other tack, and argue that Love is a poor second best to Righteousness), but he will never be able (nor ought he to desire) to dislodge that chapter from the place to which the best judgment of Europe has assigned it. Or recall the other brief passage about Love in the Romans : ' Owe no man anything, save to love one another, for he that loves his neighbour has fulfilled the Law. For the precepts, " Thou shalt not commit adultery, Thou shalt not kill, Thou shalt not steal, Thou shalt not covet," and any other commandment besides, are summed up in this word, namely, " Thou shalt love thy neighbour as thyself." Love works no evil to any man ; therefore love is the ful-

P

filment of the Law.' Who can deny the stirring nobility of this passage ? Nor will such a recognition impair our appreciation of the later saying of Akiba that the injunction in Leviticus, ' Thou shalt love thy neighbour as thyself,' is the root and supreme commandment of the entire Law.

Though the list of the virtues enumerated by Paul may hardly exceed the limits of Old Testament and Rabbinic morality, they have, it is not unreasonable to urge, a spirit and a sureness of touch, a vigour and a connectedness, which are essentially their own. They are something more than isolated and heterogeneous maxims, for they may be fairly be said to flow from the one central principle of Love, that ' more excellent way ' and ' abiding ' grace, the virtues and fruits of which are so excellently set forth in the thirteenth chapter of the 1st Corinthians.[1] Even before he wrote that famous chapter,

---

[1] Dr. Abrahams observes : ' One of the chief losses to us caused by the manner in which Rabbinic teaching has been transmitted is this lack of connectedness. If only we had a whole statement by Hillel of his views on the nature of Judaism !' (But was Hillel in his actual teaching ever ' connected ' like Paul or Philo ?)

Paul had subtly connected his sovereign ethical principle of love with his sovereign religious principle of faith, when he had said that in the religion of Christ ' neither circumcision availeth anything, nor uncircumsicion, but only faith working through and expressed in love.'

The believer, according to Paul, is a changed creature. He glories only in the cross of Christ, through which the world is crucified unto him and he unto the world. The lower, egoistic self, with its wearing strife and its vain desires, the flesh, with the passions and the lusts thereof, are now subdued and abolished. Hence the primal virtue of the Christian is what we now call unselfishness. He does not seek his own advantages, a virtue which is also described as the characteristic of love. Negatively, this unselfishness shows itself in an avoidance of all pride, vainglory, jealousy, strife, envy, insolence, boastfulness—sins against which Paul continually protests. It shows itself actively in a perfect humility, in honouring others, in modesty ; meekness is a virtue of man as it was a virtue of Christ. Again, unselfishness should lead to unity and harmony in Christian congregations. Each man must do his own part, and fulfil his own vocation. Factions, party spirit, contentiousness, disputations and rivalries are to be avoided. So we pass to the more active aspects of unselfishness, living for others, which is both the law of Christ and the imitation of Christ. Negatively, the sins which are rebuked by Paul under this head comprise covetousness and extortion, revilings, backbitings and whisperings, malignity and deceit. (His wealth of ethical language is considerable.) Positively, we get the virtues of kindness and long-suffering, brotherly affection, active helpfulness and sympathy. ' Rejoice with them that rejoice, weep with them that weep.' And again, 'Admonish the disorderly, encourage the faint-hearted, support the weak, be long-suffering toward all.' ' Bear ye one another's burdens, and so fulfil the law of Christ.' All these things lead up to that love un-

feigned which ' sums up ' the ethical commandments of God.

Devotion to Christ, the consciousness of
their high calling and of the possession of
the Holy Spirit, should exercise a definite
ethical effect upon the minds of true believers. They will put on ' the breastplate
of faith and love, and for a helmet the hope
of salvation.' The assurance of their faith,
the conviction that ' to them that love God
all things work together ' for ultimate good,
and that ' the sufferings of this present time
are not worthy to be compared with the
glory which shall be revealed,' give them a
wonderful power of endurance in the midst
of earthly tribulation. Nay, more, they
supply them with peace—' the peace of God
which passeth all understanding '—with a
grand content, and even with an ineffable
joy. Several times over does Paul speak
of his own happiness in suffering and per-
secution ; and it is remarkable, as we have
seen, with what emphasis he speaks of 'joy'
as an element in Christian character. It is
the second fruit of the spirit in that long

list of which the first fruit is love, and in the moral code in the Epistle to the Romans, 'joy in hope' precedes, and implies, 'patience in tribulation.' And we get it again among the famous paradoxes which describe the spirit in which Paul lived through his wonderful missionary life.

Since the body is the dwelling-place of the Holy Spirit, so that each believer is himself a visible sanctuary of God, purity in body and purity in mind are the virtues which befit so high a privilege and responsibility. Paul gives to his diatribes against all sexual impurity, as well as against drunkenness, debauchery and lasciviousness, this deep spiritual foundation. The character which he seeks to train is one of simplicity, sincerity and truth. Hence his not unfrequent use of such words as 'unblameable,' 'harmless,' 'sincerity,' 'pureness,' and 'simplicity.' These virtues are necesary for that ethical sanctification to which the new life of the believer must lead. ' For God called us not for uncleanness, but in sanctification,' that is, to live holy lives.

There must be no *Hintergedanken*, no taint
of selfish motive, in the service of Christ.
The whole man is required. Hence the
remarkable way in which, following the
Rabbinic difference between almsgiving and
the doing of kindnesses, Paul distinguishes
between the higher and lower charity : ' If
I bestow all my goods to feed the poor, but
have not love, it profiteth me nothing.'

Paul's ideal Christian must be, as he says,
' wise unto that which is good, simple unto
that which is evil,' or as he elsewhere says,
' in malice a babe, but in mind a man.' It is
noticeable that seemliness is considered a
fruit of love, and everybody quotes the
phrase, ' Let all things be done decently
and in order.' Yet while a certain grace and
even pliability of character are commended,
the believer must show firmess and immovable constancy when principles are
involved. Paul's own life testified to this
need, and he gives counsel corresponding :
' Be ye steadfast, immovable, always
abounding in the work of the Lord.' So,
too, a few sentences later at the close of the

same Epistle : ' Watch ye, stand fast in the faith, quit you like men, be strong.' To which, however, he adds, coming back again once more to the sovereign principle of all, ' Let all that ye do be done in love.'

For my own part I see no reason why Judaism cannot follow the precedent of its early teachers, and continue to proclaim the necessity both of love *and* of righteousness. As to the primacy I will not argue, but so far as Paul and love are concerned, I am disposed to agree with a story about a certain Jew which Dean Stanley quotes from a sermon of John Wesley. It may be worth while to add that Wesley says nothing about this Jew showing any inclination to adopt the specific tenets of dogmatic Christianity. Here are his words : 'Nothing is more common than to find even those who deny the authority of the Holy Scriptures, yet affirming, " This is my religion : that which is described in the thirteenth chapter of the Corinthians," Nay, even a Jew, Dr. Nunes, a Spanish physician, then settled at Savannah, in Georgia, used to say,

with great earnestness, " that Paul of
Tarsus was one of the finest writers I have
ever read. I wish the thirteenth chapter
of his first letter to the Corinthians were
wrote in letters of gold ; and I wish every
Jew were to carry it with him wherever he
went." He judged (and herein he certainly
judged right) that this single chapter contained the whole of true religion.'

For all his fervid teaching about love, it
cannot be said that Paul shows any lack of
zeal in the cause of righteousness. His
hatred of vice, his passion for integrity and
holy living, are patent to every reader of his
letters. Moreover, they are essentially
Jewish. They show that he, too, no less
than his Master, may be regarded as following, in this respect, in the footsteps of
the Prophets. In spite of his stress upon
faith, he shows (where controversy about
the Law does not come in) scarcely less stress
upon works. He is guilty, no doubt, of a
certain inconsistency. That faith does not
avail without works can easily be maintained out of Paul's own words. The un-

conscious Rabbinic resolve to establish a harmony between faith and works is justified by the necessity, which Paul himself seems sometimes to have felt, of rejecting an absolutely unqualified reliance on faith. The Christian after death will be judged by his deeds. ' For all of us have to stand without disguise before the judgment seat of Christ, that every one may receive the result of his life in the body, according to what he has done, whether good or bad.' God ' will render to every man according to his works.' Dr. Menzies observes : ' That there is inconsistency between the doctrine of justification by faith alone and this doctrine of a final judgment of men according to their actions, it is difficult to deny. On the one hand, Paul teaches a judgment on moral grounds, which applies to Christians as well as to Jews and Gentiles ; on the other hand, the saved are with him the called, the elect only, and those who accept the new method of justification by faith.'[1] We shall not,

---

[1] The second Epistle to the Corinthians, edited by Dr. Allan Menzies (1912), p. 37.

however, by any means object to this inconsistency, for it enables Paul to hint here and there that even for non-Christian Jews and non-Christian Gentiles there may perchance be some method, on the one hand, of attaining to righteousness, on the other hand, of finding salvation. ' When Gentiles who have not the Law do by nature the commands of the Law, these, having not the Law, are a law unto themselves, in that they show the works of the Law written in their hearts.' And, so far as the Jews are concerned, there are those noble and prophetic words (with which we may perhaps not unfitly bring this essay to a close) : ' He is not a Jew who is one outwardly ; neither is that circumcision which is outward in the flesh : but he is a Jew who is one inwardly, and circumcision is that of the heart, in the spirit, not in the letter ; whose praise is not of men, but of God.'[1]

---

[1] Dr. Abrahams observes : ' A Jew should, I think, put some of the clauses a little differently. He should say : Being a Jew outwardly, let me see to it that I am also a Jew inwardly. We may derive from Paul much enthusiasm for the Spirit. But it is Judaism which must instruct us how to infuse the letter *with* the spirit, so that a man, body and soul, may be made one and whole in his desire to love and reverence God.'

APPENDIX

COMPARATIVELY few persons read, I fear,
the invaluable *Revue* in which, every two
months, M. Loisy pours out the results of
his immense learning and admirable impartiality. The great scholar seems now
to have reached a position of complete
detachment from which, as from a lofty
height, he surveys, with supreme serenity,
all the religions of the past. Truth is his
single aim, and in which direction truth
lies seems to be, so far as he is concerned,
wholly indifferent. He is thus raised far
above all those scholars and students,
whether Protestant, Catholic, or Jewish,
who obviously do care about results, and
who, however much they may try to be
impartial, and to look at the facts with
absolute objectivity, are yet unable to do
so. It may be interesting, and is surely
worth while, to collect here some passages in

which M. Loisy deals with the relation of Paul to the ' mystery religions ' and with the arguments of scholars such as Clemen, or Wendland, or Deissmann, or Schweitzer (and here one might add Kennedy),who seek to show that Paul borrowed little or nothing from the ' mysteries ' or from ' mystery ' thought, and that his own religious creations were therefore arrived at wholly independently of them.

(1) ' Sur les rapports du Christianisme avec les religions de mystères M. Wendland (in his splendid book " Die hellenistisch-rômische Kultur in ihren Beziehungen zu Judentum und Christentum ") n'est par très explicite, ou plutôt il demeure très circonspect . . . Il nous dit bien que Paul a connu le vocabulaire et les idées des religions syncrétistes, des cultes orientaux hellénisés, et il définit fort heureusement le moyen de cette influence sur l'esprit de Paul : pas d'emprunt mécanique, accidentel, réfléchi, mais transformation spontanée de tout un ensemble de sentiments et d'idées dans une conscience forte-

ment pénétrée de l'atmosphère des religions
dont il s'agit.   Rien n'est plus vrai : mais
ce n'est pas toute la vérité.   On nous parle
toujours de conscience religieuse, comme si
Paul n'avait été qu'une conscience, et même
une conscience moderne, voire protestante.
On oublie toujours l'intelligence mobile et
pénétrable, l'imagination sensible et sur-
excitée, le cerveau en travail, capables
d'opérer parfois très vite (témoin le fait
de la conversion) les plus déconcertantes
évolutions.   On doit compter avec cet
esprit de Paul autant qu'avec sa conscience
et même davantage ; car cet esprit était la
lumière et le guide de cette conscience.
Dans ce qu'on appelle expérience religieuse
de Paul part est à faire, très grande, à ce
mouvement d'une pensée fébrile, prompte
à s'assimiler même—peut-être devrait-on
dire : d'abord—ce qu'elle combat.   Cette
extrême mobilité d'un esprit visionnaire,
qui doit servir à expliquer le fait capital de
la vie de Paul, à savoir sa conversion, pourrait également servir à expliquer certains
éléments de sa doctrine et même de sa

conscience religieuse, par exemple sa conception de l'universalité du salut et le sentiment de sa propre vocation auprès des païens. Ni de l'une ni de l'autre il ne semble qu'on ait donné jusqu'à présent d'explications pleinement satisfaisantes. M. W., qui accentue peut-être un peu plus que de raison l'universalisme de l'Évangile, ne laisse pas de reconnaître que la prédicaîion de Jésus avait un double aspect, et qu'elle pouvait aboutir à une rechute dans le judaïsme aussi bien qu'à la victoire de la tendance universaliste qu'elle portait en soi. Paul aurait déterminé la direction de l'avenir. Mais comment Paul y est-il arrivé ? Comment Paul y a-t-il été amené ? Certes, ce n'est pas pour avoir perçu dans l'Évangile de Jésus l'élément universel qu'y discerne M. W. Tout le monde sait que l'Apôtre ne prétend à rien moins qu'à interpréter la prédication du Christ. C'est le Christ immortel qui lui a révélé l'économie de salut qu'il prêche, et c'est au même Christ qu'il rapporte sa vocation. Osera-t-on le contredire sur ce point essentiel ? On est

tellement habitué à le contredire discrète-
ment qu'on a fini par ne plus s'en apercevoir.
Or c'est là que gît le mystère de la conversion, et il s'explique,—qu'on me par-
donne le jeu de mots,—si l'on veut bien voir
que ce fut la conversion à un mystère, à
cette religion même du salut acquis à tous
par la mort du Christ et par la foi à ce Christ
mort et ressuscité. C'est cette idée-là que
Paul a eue dès le commencement : or il ne
la devait ni au judaïsme, ni aux premiers
fidèles de Jésus. Ne la devrait-il pas aux
mystères, et sa conversion ne consisterait-
elle pas dans l'application qu'il a faite au
Christ des principes qui caractérisaient les
cultes de mystères, salut proposé aux
croyants de toute nation qui participeraient
par la foi et les rites de l'initiation aux
aventures mystiques, parfois à la mort et à
la résurrection d'un héros divin ? Il est
bien difficile de ne pas l'admettre et conséquemment de ne point placer l'influence des
mystères à l'origine même du christianisme,
dans la conversion de l'homme qui a con-
tribué plus que personne à faire de l'Évan-

Q

gile une religion et une religion universelle,
au lieu d'une petite secte sans avenir dans
le judaïsme où elle était née. La pression
des événements ne rend pas suffisamment
compte de l'évolution du christianisme
primitif ; car la prédication aux païens ne
fut pas une nécessité du christianisme
naissant, et Paul lui-même a compris la
chose tout autrement. Il serait au moins
risqué de soutenir qu'il a imaginé sa théorie
de l'universalité du salut pour justifier les
missions déjà faites et les conversions ac-
complies chez les païens, quand lui-même dit
expressément et clairement le contraire. On
n'a pas lieu d'alléguer contre ce témoignage
formel celui des Actes, où il semble toujours
que Paul ne prêche aux païens que lorsque
les Juifs le chassent. M. W. nous apprend
à suspecter ici le point de vue systématique
des Actes.'[1]

(2) 'Que le chapitre vii. de l'Épitre aux
Romains représente une expérience religieuse et morale toute personelle de Paul
encore juif, et même de sa première jeunesse,

[1] Revue d'histoire et de littérature religieuses, vol. iii. 1912,
p. 566, 567.

M. Deissmann (in his Paulus : Eine kultur
—und religionsgeschichtliche Skizze, 1911)
n'est pas le premier à le soutenir, et l'on
s'expose grandement, en le contestant, à
scandaliser à peu près tous les théologiens
protestants. Il faudra pourtant en rabattre
aussi beaucoup de cette prétendue expérience, qui est avant tout une argumenta-
tion contre le salut par la Loi, argumenta-
tion qui n'a jamais pu prendre dans l'esprit
d'un pharisien la forme que nous lui voyons ;
la part d'expérience préalable à la conversion doit être beaucoup réduite, et il n'y a
pas lieu de la transformer en drame
psychologique d'une particulière intensité
qui aurait troublé la conscience de Paul
enfant. . . . . . On nous a souvent
fabriqué un Paul plus ou moins moderne,
qui se serait formé peu à peu sa christologie
et toute sa doctrine sous la pression des
événements quand il fut converti. Paul dit
positivement le contraire, et il n'a pas dû
se tromper radicalement sur son propre cas.
Le grand mérite de M. D. est de montrer
Paul tel qu'il se donne ; ainsi le comprend-

il mieux que ceux qui altèrent le témoignage de l'Apôtre. Mais le problème reste. D'où cela vient-il ?

A cette question les effusions pathétiques de M. D. n'apportent pas de réponse. Il lui arrive bien de dire que l'ouvrage de M. Reitzenstein sur les cultes de mystères fournit des termes de comparaison qui peuvent servir à expliquer certaines locutions et même certaines idées pauliniennes. Mais il ne va pas plus loin. Il se contente de prouver fort longuement—ce qui n'a rien d'inutile pour les théologiens,—que les idées de Paul ne sont pas coordonnées en système, que ce sont des formes ou des aspects de sa foi, des impressions vivantes avec lesquelles on a construit plus tard des théories. Cette thèse renferme une grande part de vérité, mais elle comporte aussi une grande lacune. M. D. soutient, et sans doute il a raison de soutenir, que le langage de Paul était intelligible pour ceux à qui il s'adressait. Le langage et les idées qu'il traduit ne sont donc pas l'expression rigoureusement personnelle d'expériences qui auraient été particulières à Paul, ou même aux seuls chrétiens, aux païens convertis à la foi de Paul. La question serait d'abord de savoir s'il a jamais existé, s'il peut exister dans l'humanité des expériences psychologiques tellement personnelles qu'elles ne doivent rien au milieu où vit l'individu en qui elles se produisent. En un sens, elles doivent à ce milieu quelque chose de tout ce qu'elles sont. Et dans le cas présent, si Paul réussit à se faire entendre des païens, c'est qu'il a conçu lui-même en païen le salut qu'il leur prêche. En fait, la religion qu'il leur annonce ressemble de tout point aux religions de mystère qui commençaient alors la conquête du monde romain : d'abord c'est une assurance d'immortalité bienheureuse, ce que n'étaient pas les anciens cultes nationaux, ce que n'était même pas le judaïsme officiel, mais ce qu'étaient les religions de mystère ; de plus, comme dans les mystères orientaux, la garantie d'immortalité se fonde sur la communion à un héros divin souffrant, mourant et ressuscitant ; ·par les rites de l'initiation l'on participe mystiquement à son épreuve, à sa mort, et lui étant identifié ainsi dans le sacrement, on ne peut manquer de lui être associé dans la gloire de son immortalité (se rappeler comment Paul argumente sur le sujet de la résurrection); enfin, comme dans les cultes de mystère, on est sauvé par la grâce divine, et en même temps par la foi, par la foi au dieu qui sauve, qui sauve par la mort. Toutes ces idées que Paul rabbinise quelque peu, tout en accentuant leur portée morale, Paul ne les doit pas au rabbinisme. Car cela ne vient pas du judaïsme, cela est tout autre chose que l'Évangile de Jésus. Paul a connu les cultes de mystères, certains cultes, il s'est pénétré de leur esprit dès avant sa conversion, et cette circonstance même explique en quelque manière sa conversion, explique sa vocation. Car, précisement, les cultes de mystère offrent le salut à tout venant sans distinction de nationalité, tandis que l'Évangile de Jésus ne s'adressait qu'aux juifs. En vérité, ce n'est pas assez, pour expliquer la mentalité de Paul, que de mon-

trer en lui, avec M. D., le juif nourri de la
version des Septante et pénétré de son
esprit. Tout bien considéré, le miracle qui
a fait de Paul un disciple et un apôtre de
Jésus, ce n'est pas l'éblouissement qui l'a
renversé sur le chemin de Damas, c'est
l'éclair jaillissant en son cerveau troublé,
qui lui a fait voir dans le crucifié du Gol-
gotha, dans le Christ des apôtres galiléens,
l'être divin qui était venu sauver le monde
par sa mort. Et l'on peut trouver que cette
idée-là porte sa marque d'origine.'[1]

(3) ' La question de l'influence des cultes
de mystères sur le christianisme primitif se
ramène pour M. Clemen à une série de petits
problèmes, à savoir si telle croyance ou tel
mot caractéristique, tel rite ont été emprun-
tés à tel ou tel mystère selon qu'il nous
peut être connu. Tel était le point de vue
de sa *Religionsgeschichtliche Erklärung des
Neuen Testaments*, publiée en 1909 : tel
reste celui de la très érudite brochure qu'il
vient de publier sur le même sujet (*Der
Einfluss der Mysterienreligionen auf das*

---

[1]Revue, vol. iii. 1912, p. 573-574.

älteste Christentum, 1913). Or il ne semble pas que le problème soit ainsi posé tel qu'il est dans ses véritables termes, dans sa réelle ampleur.

Il s'agit en effet de savoir comment l'Évangile de Jésus, c'est-à-dire l'annonce à Israel de l'accomplissement prochain du règne de Dieu, avec Jésus pour Christ-roi, est devenu le christianisme, c'est-à-dire une religion distincte du judaïsme, dont l'Évangile n'était que la couronnement, religion qui est constituée en économie de salut universel, avec un mythe de salut,—car la théorie paulinienne de la rédemption n'est pas autre chose, et Paul lui-même la qualifie expressément de " gnose " et de " mystère," —et des rites mystiques par lesquels les fidèles régénérés sont unis en esprit au Christ immortel, véritable esprit ou dieu du mystère chrétien. La question est là tout entière, car tout le reste est accessoire, et il importe assez peu de savoir si tel trait particulier, par exemple l'interprétation paulinienne du baptême ou de l'eucharistie, a été plus ou moins suggérée par tel mystère

plutôt que par tel autre. Sur ce dernier
terrain il ne peut pas manquer de régner
beaucoup d'incertitudes, car on connaît fort
mal et l'aire d'expansion géographique des
cultes des différents mystères au premier
siècle après J.-C., et l'état de leurs doctrines
et de leurs pratiques, et dans quelle mesure
les écrivains du Nouveau Testament ont
pu en être instruits, dans quelles conditions
s'est formé le premier et le plus grand
des gnostiques chrétiens, celui qu'on appelle
l'Apôtre des Gentils, saint Paul, Saul
dit Paul, de Tarse en Cilicie. M. Clemen
abuse vraiment de ces incertitudes, et
parce qu'en de nombreux détails l'influence
des mystères n'est pas évidente, il pense
avoir fermé toutes les portes par lesquelles
le paganisme aurait eu prise sur le
christianisme primitif, il croit pouvoir con-
clure en toute sécurité que l'influence des
mystères sur le christianisme primitif n'a
été que superficielle, accessoire, que le
christianisme primitif est plutôt une *Anti-
mysterienreligion* qu'une *Mysterienreligion*.
Par malheur il n'a oublié que le point

essentiel ; l'Évangile n'était pas une religion ; comment l'est-il devenu ? Comment l'annonce du royaume de Dieu avec
le Christ-roi est-elle devenue une économie
de salut par la foi au divin Crucifié et l'union
mystique au Christ immortel ? Cette
religion-là, qui est le christianisme de Paul,
cette religion-là n'est ni le judaïsme ni
l'Evangile de Jésus. D'où vient-elle ? De
toute évidence c'est la forme qu'a prise le
judaïsme évangélique pour s'adapter au
milieu païen où il s'est implanté ; de tout
évidence cette transformation aboutit à une
économie de salut qui ressemble, et pour ce
qui est de la croyance et pour que ce qui est
du sens attaché aux rites essentiels, aux
religions de mystères. De toute évidence
c'est par l'influence du milieu païen que le
christianisme a pris ce caractère. De tout
évidence ce caractère n'est point quelque
chose de superficiel, mais quelque chose de
très profond, car il n'y va de rien moins que
du Christ-Sauveur et des sacrements chrétiens. Pour l'historien qui n'a dans cette
affaire aucun intérêt de foi, l'influence

réelle, profonde,—d'ailleures inévitable, et sans laquelle le christianisme n'aurait pas existé,—du paganisme et spécialement des mystères païens ne peut pas faire doute, et ce qui est à déterminer, ce sont les conditions, c'est le mode de cette influence.

M. C. s'est fait la partie belle en supposant que cette influence n'avait pu consister qu'en un tas plus ou moins considérable d'emprunts spéciaux, matériels en quelque façon, de morceaux de paganisme brutalement transplantés dans la prédication chrétienne. Beaucoup de ceux qu'il réfute ont eu l'air de l'entendre eux-mêmes ainsi ; il s'ensuit seulement que sa réfutation ne manque pas de valeur relative. Mais ne doit-on pas se représenter le christianisme comme reprenant sous une autre forme, dans d'autres conditions, l'œuvre du judaïsme hellénistique, une transposition du monothéisme juif, par assimilation, non par simple ingestion, d'éléments venus du paganisme ? Et comme le christianisme, à la différence du judaïsme philonien par example, était un mouvement essentielle-

ment religieux, non philosophique, n'est-il
pas naturel qu'il se soit assimilé les éléments
les plus vivants des religions païennes, et
qu'il se les soit assimilés par la puissance du
sentiment mystique, non par un travail de
réflexion, par l'élan d'âmes plus ou moins
pénétrées de la mystique du paganisme,
non par l'étude des textes et pratiques du
paganisme ? Est-ce que dans l'àme ardente
et visionnaire d'un saint Paul les idées
religieuses du milieu où il vivait, où il
s'agitait, pouvaient tomber en vain ? Est-ce
qu'un beau jour l'idèe du Christ-Jésus, qu'il
avait combattue, ne se trouva pas dominer
sa pensée ?   Et croira-t-on que ce fut par
hasard que cette idée se trouva par la même
occasion muée en celle du Christ sauveur
des hommes par la mort de la croix ? N'est-
ce pas que Paul, qui connaissait beaucoup de
dieux et de sauveurs et de seigneurs, aux-
quels il ne voulait pas croire, se créant par
son refus persistant le besoin de croire à
l'un d'eux, s'avisa tout à coup,—dans un
coup de vision,—que Jésus était le Christ
parce qu'il était le Sauveur, le vrai, institué

par le Dieu unique, et que la mort de la croix était précisément l'acte par lequel il avait *sauvé* le monde ? Poser à ce propos la question d'emprunt est presque ridicule. Ce n'est pas délibérément que Paul a placé le Christ dans une fonction analogue à celle des dieux de mystère ; il a pensé le mettre et il l'a mis beaucoup plus haut, bien que, s'il n'eût connu que la tradition juive palestinienne, s'il n'eût remué dans son esprit des conceptions païennes, il n'eût jamais compris ainsi le rôle du Messie ni le salut apporté par lui. Influence et emprunt sont deux. Il peut y avoir influence sans emprunt formel.

Mais ce n'est le lieu de traiter à fond le sujet que M. C. a envisagé par ses petits côtés. Disons seulement que la même remarque est à faire sur beaucoup des points de détail que touche M. C. Parce que tel trait qu'il examine ne se retrouve pas identique dans le christianisme et dans le mystère païen où on le recontre, M. C. nie l'emprunt. Mais là aussi l'influence est possible sans qu'il y ait eu emprunt con-

scient. On peut même dire que tous les
éléments de la mystique païenne que le
christianisme primitif s'est assimilés, il les
a transformés en se le assimilant. M. C.
peut donc nier l'emprunt ; il ne prouve pas
que l'influence païenne n'ait pas existé, que
le christianisme ait tiré ces éléments de lui-
même. Ni le christianisme n'est un mystère
comme les autres, ni les éléments qu'il tient
des mystères ne sont restés simplement ce
qu'ils étaient dans ceux-ci. La foi mono-
théiste leur donne une autre consistance, la
personne du Christ leur donne plus de vie,
son Évangile plus de valeur morale. Le
christianisme reste malgré tout une exploita-
tion du syncrétisme païen pour le compte
du monothéisme juif. Par là il se différencie
nettement du gnosticisme, avec lequel le
christianisme primitif, surtout chez Paul, a
tant d'affinité, mais qui n'est pas autre
chose, si on l'entend bien, qu'une exploita-
tion du christianisme pour le compte du
syncrétisme païen.'[1]

(4) 'Les objections de M. Schweitzer (in

---

[1]Revue, vol. iv., 1913, p. 477-480.

his fascinating book, Die Geschichte der Paulinischen Forschung von der Reformation bis auf die Gegenwart, 1911) aux savants qui admettent une influence des mystères sur les croyances de saint Paul portent surtout contre ceux qui supposent de véritables emprunts, une exacte conformité entre les croyances des mystères et la conception paulinienne du salut. Or il n'est pas douteux qu'aucun mystère ne concevait le rôle du dieu sauveur comme Paul a compris celui de son Christ. Mais la question pourrait bien ne se poser pas dans ces termes-là. Il s'agit de savoir si Paul (c'est-à-dire le mouvement de foi dont il est pour nous le représentant le plus connu), qui conçoit le rôle du Christ et l'objet de l'Évangile autrement que Jésus lui-même ne les a compris, est arrivé à sa conception du salut, à l'idée qu'il se fait des rites chrétiens du baptême et de l'eucharistie, sans aucune influence des notions qui étaient à la base des mystères, passion divine suivie de résurrection, fait primordial typique et efficace d'immortalité pour ceux qui y sont

mystiquement associés par les rites de
l'initiation. Or qu'une telle conception ne
soit ni juive ni évangélique, c'est certain ;
que Paul l'ait eue, ce n'est pas douteux ;
qu'elle se soit formée en lui par l'influence
du milieu où elle régnait avant lui, c'est ce
qui paraît évident. Paul n'a copié aucun
mythe, imité aucun mystère, mais, devant
le paganisme, dans le monde païen, vivant
dans une atmosphère païenne dont les idées
le pénétraient malgré lui, il a conçu le salut
chrétien à l'instar des économies de salut
qu'étaient déjà en ce temps-là les mystères
de Mithra, d'Isis, de la Mère, d'Éleusis, dont
il est superflu de lui dénier toute connaissance générale, comme il serait gratuit de lui
prêter la connaissance réfléchie, spéciale,
étudiee d'un seul. Paul a connu la religiosité païenne du monde méditerranéen,
et il a interprété l'Évangile avec et contre
cette religiosité, faisant du Christ le véritable
sauveur et de sa mort le vrai principe de
salut.'[1]

---

[1]Revue, vol. iv , 1913, p. 486.

THE JEWISH PEOPLE

HISTORY • RELIGION • LITERATURE

AN ARNO PRESS COLLECTION

Agus, Jacob B. **The Evolution of Jewish Thought:** From Biblical Times to the Opening of the Modern Era. 1959

Ber of Bolechow. **The Memoirs of Ber of Bolechow (1723-1805).** Translated from the Original Hebrew MS. with an Introduction, Notes and a Map by M[ark] Vishnitzer. 1922

Berachya. **The Ethical Treatises of Berachya, Son of Rabbi Natronai Ha-Nakdan:** Being the Compendium and the Masref. Now edited for the First Time from MSS. at Parma and Munich with an English Translation, Introduction, Notes, etc. by Hermann Gollancz. 1902

Bloch, Joseph S. **My Reminiscences.** 1923

Bokser, Ben Zion, **Pharisaic Judaism in Transition:** R. Eliezer the Great and Jewish Reconstruction After the War with Rome. 1935

Dalman, Gustaf. **Jesus Christ in the Talmud, Midrash, Zohar, and the Liturgy of the Synagogue.** Together with an Introductory Essay by Heinrich Laible. Translated and Edited by A. W. Streane. 1893

Daube, David. **The New Testament and Rabbinic Judaism.** 1956

Davies, W. D. **Christian Origins and Judaism.** 1962

Engelman, Uriah Zevi. **The Rise of the Jew in the Western World:** A Social and Economic History of the Jewish People of Europe. Foreword by Niles Carpenter. 1944

Epstein, Louis M. **The Jewish Marriage Contract:** A Study in the Status of the Woman in Jewish Law. 1927

Facets of Medieval Judaism. 1973. New Introduction by Seymour Siegel

The Foundations of Jewish Life: Three Studies. 1973

Franck, Adolph. **The Kabbalah, or, The Religious Philosophy of the Hebrews.** Revised and Enlarged Translation [from the French] by Dr. I. Sossnitz. 1926

Goldman, Solomon. **The Jew and The Universe.** 1936

Gordon, A. D. **Selected Essays.** Translated by Frances Burnce from the Hebrew Edition by N. Teradyon and A. Shohat, with a Biographical Sketch by E. Silberschlag. 1938

Ha-Am, Achad (Asher Ginzberg). **Ten Essays on Zionism and Judaism.** Translated from the Hebrew by Leon Simon. 1922. New Introduction by Louis Jacobs

Halevi, Jehudah. **Selected Poems of Jehudah Halevi.** Translated into English by Nina Salaman, Chiefly from the Critical Text Edited by Heinrich Brody. 1924

Heine, Heinrich. **Heinrich Heine's Memoir:** From His Works, Letters, and Conversations. Edited by Gustav Karpeles; English Translation by Gilbert Cannan. 1910. Two volumes in one

Heine, Heinrich. **The Prose Writings of Heinrich Heine.**
Edited, with an Introduction, by Havelock Ellis. 1887

Hirsch, Emil G[ustav]. **My Religion.** Compilation and
Biographical Introduction by Gerson B. Levi. **Including
The Crucifixion Viewed from a Jewish Standpoint:** A Lecture
Delivered by Invitation Before the "Chicago Institute for
Morals, Religion and Letters." 1925/1908

Hirsch, W. **Rabbinic Psychology:** Beliefs about the Soul
in Rabbinic Literature of the Talmudic Period. 1947

Historical Views of Judaism: Four Selections. 1973

Ibn Gabirol, Solomon. **Selected Religious Poems of Solomon Ibn
Gabirol.** Translated into English Verse by Israel Zangwill
from a Critical Text Edited by Israel Davidson. 1923

Jacobs, Joseph. **Jesus as Others Saw Him:** A Retrospect
A. D. 54. Preface by Israel Abrahams; Introductory Essay by
Harry A. Wolfson. 1925

Judaism and Christianity: Selected Accounts, 1892-1962.
1973. New Preface and Introduction by Jacob B. Agus

Kohler, Kaufmann. **The Origins of the Synagogue and
The Church.** Edited, with a Biographical Essay by H. G. Enelow.
1929

Maimonides Octocentennial Series, Numbers I-IV. 1935

Mann, Jacob. **The Responsa of the Babylonian Geonim as a
Source of Jewish History.** 1917-1921

Maritain, Jacques. **A Christian Looks at the Jewish Question.** 1939

Marx, Alexander. **Essays in Jewish Biography.** 1947

Mendelssohn, Moses. **Phaedon; or, The Death of Socrates.**
Translated from the German [by Charles Cullen]. 1789

Modern Jewish Thought: Selected Issues, 1889-1966. 1973.
New Introduction by Louis Jacobs

Montefiore, C[laude] G. **Judaism and St. Paul:** Two Essays. 1914

Montefiore, C[laude] G. **Some Elements of the Religious
Teaching of Jesus According to the Synoptic Gospels.** Being
the Jowett Lectures for 1910. 1910

Radin, Max. **The Jews Amongs the Greeks and Romans.** 1915

Ruppin, Arthur. **The Jews in the Modern World.** With an
Introduction by L. B. Namier. 1934

Smith, Henry Preserved. **The Bible and Islam;** or, The Influence
of the Old and New Testaments on the Religion of Mohammed.
Being the Ely Lectures for 1897. 1897

Stern, Nathan. **The Jewish Historico-Critical School of the
Nineteenth Century.** 1901

Walker, Thomas [T.] **Jewish Views of Jesus:** An Introduction
and an Appreciation. 1931. New Introduction by Seymour Siegel

Walter, H. **Moses Mendelssohn:** Critic and Philosopher. 1930

Wiener, Leo. **The History of Yiddish Literature in the
Nineteenth Century.** 1899

Wise, Isaac M. **Reminiscences.** Translated from the German and
Edited, with an Introduction by David Philipson. 1901